ISSUE 15, JULY 2022

AUSTRALIAN FOREIGN AFFAIRS

Contributors

Nicole Curato is an associate professor of sociology at the Centre for Deliberative Democracy and Global Governance at the University of Canberra.

Sheila Fitzpatrick is a renowned historian of the Soviet Union and modern Russia.

Allan Gyngell is national president of the Australian Institute of International Affairs.

Kishore Mahbubani is a Singaporean academic, diplomat and geopolitical consultant.

Adam Ni is director of the China Policy Centre in Canberra.

Mercedes Page formerly worked for the Australian Department of Foreign Affairs and Trade. She is a fellow with the Schmidt Futures International Strategy Forum.

Sebastian Strangio is a journalist and author and is currently the South-East Asia Editor of *The Diplomat*.

Thom Woodroofe is chief of staff to the president and CEO of the Asia Society and a fellow of the Asia Society Policy Institute, where he works on climate policy and diplomacy.

Australian Foreign Affairs is published three times a year by Schwartz Books Pty Ltd. Publisher: Morry Schwartz. ISBN 978-1-76064-3461 ISSN 2208-5912 ALL RIGHTS RESERVED. No part of this publication may be reproduced, stored in a retrieval system, or transmitted in any form by any means, electronic, mechanical, photocopying, recording or otherwise, without the prior consent of the publishers. Essays, reviews and correspondence © retained by the authors. Subscriptions – 1 year print & digital auto-renew (3 issues): $49.99 within Australia incl. GST. 1 year print and digital subscription (3 issues): $59.99 within Australia incl. GST. 2 year print & digital (6 issues): $114.99 within Australia incl. GST. 1 year digital only auto-renew: $29.99. Payment may be made by MasterCard, Visa or Amex, or by cheque made out to Schwartz Books Pty Ltd. Payment includes postage and handling. To subscribe, fill out the form inside this issue, subscribe online at www.australianforeignaffairs.com, email subscribe@australianforeignaffairs.com or phone 1800 077 514 / 61 3 9486 0288. Correspondence should be addressed to: The Editor, Australian Foreign Affairs, 22–24 Northumberland Street, Collingwood, VIC, 3066 Australia Phone: 61 3 9486 0288 / Fax: 61 3 9486 0244 Email: enquiries@australianforeignaffairs.com Editor: Jonathan Pearlman. Deputy Editor: Kirstie Innes-Will. Associate Editor: Chris Feik. Consulting Editor: Allan Gyngell. Digital Editor and Marketing: Georgia Mill. Editorial intern: Emma Hoy. Management: Elisabeth Young. Subscriptions: Iryna Byelyayeva and Sam Perazzo. Publicity: Anna Lensky. Design: Peter Long. Production Coordination: Marilyn de Castro. Typesetting: Typography Studio. Cover photograph: Andrea Domeniconi / Alamy. Printed in Australia by McPherson's Printing Group.

Editor's Note

OUR UNSTABLE NEIGHBOURHOOD

For his first bilateral visit as prime minister, Anthony Albanese, travelled, as expected, to Indonesia.

But this thirty-year-old rite of passage for Australian leaders must amount to more than ticking off an item on an incoming prime ministerial to-do list. Unfortunately, these trips have not ensured that those who undertake them return with a lasting sense of the relationship's importance. During his visit to Jakarta as a newly sworn-in leader in 2018, Scott Morrison spoke of bringing ties to a "new level". Six weeks later, he flagged relocating Australia's embassy in Israel from Tel Aviv to Jerusalem – a move that caused disquiet in Indonesia, the world's largest Muslim-majority nation. Two years later, when Morrison pushed for an inquiry into the origins of COVID-19, he contacted the leaders of countries such as the United States and France, but not Indonesia.

Beyond Indonesia, the grouping of countries that forms Australia's immediate regional neighbourhood – South-East Asia – has, in recent years, been subject to similar patterns of neglect. Australian aid to the region has declined since 2014, though support has been lifted during the COVID pandemic. Prime ministerial visits to most South-East Asian countries have been rare and irregular; the last leader to make a standalone visit to the Philippines – a nation of 115 million people – was John Howard, in 2003.

Yet Australia's declining focus on South-East Asia has occurred at a time when the region's importance has spiked. In 2020, the combined gross domestic product of the ASEAN countries was US$3 trillion, having more than tripled in fifteen years. South-East Asia has become central to the competition between China and the United States, as the contest between these powers has focused on the great shipping lanes that connect the Indian Ocean to Asia and the Pacific.

But countries in South-East Asia tend to view China, and the consequences of China's rise, very differently to Australia. Their approaches are not monolithic but tend to diverge from Australia's for similar reasons – they are closer to China (some are neighbours), and have longer memories of ties with it, including histories that extend into the days when it was last a great trading empire. Unlike Australia, they have provided the battlegrounds for previous wars between great powers, which shapes their views of the rivalries between the great powers of today.

The Albanese government has committed to improving ties across South-East Asia, including increasing aid and appointing a roving ambassador to the region. Significantly, Australia's foreign minister, Penny Wong, has suggested that Australia's approach must be based on an appreciation of the region's outlook. In a speech at the Australian National University in 2021, she said South-East Asian countries "don't want to choose between the great powers – but they want to exercise their own agency in how the region is being reshaped". Wong, it should be noted, is the first foreign minister who was born in the region. She told the Lowy Institute in 2019: "Southeast Asia is not just our region; it is where I was born. I grew up with stories of the fall of Singapore, the occupation of Malaya and the unique American contribution to peace in the Pacific."

But the test for the Albanese government will be, as always, whether its commitment to the region endures as other political and international challenges arise. Wong had hoped her first bilateral visit would be to Indonesia and Malaysia, her birthplace. But China's Pacific outreach sent her rushing to Fiji, three days after her swearing in.

Developments in the Pacific have highlighted the danger of waiting for trouble before stepping up our diplomacy. Australia must start developing and improving relations with South-East Asia now. Albanese should visit the region, regularly, and build meaningful contacts and partnerships there, as should the rest of government and the business community. But, to succeed, Australia must first understand the outlooks of our potential partners in the region, and the causes of their concerns and anxieties – and then the reasons for our neglect, and the ways in which we can enhance ties and remain committed, permanently.

Jonathan Pearlman

TESTING GROUND

A new statecraft for South-East Asia

Allan Gyngell

South-East Asia is the hyphen in the Indo-Pacific. Shaped by the great river systems of the Mekong, the Irrawaddy and the Salween, the subcontinental bulk of the mainland states of Thailand, Myanmar, Vietnam, Cambodia and Laos fractures into the archipelagos and islands of Malaysia, Singapore, Brunei, Indonesia and the Philippines. Linking the Indian and Pacific oceans, the Malacca, Sunda and Lombok straits are critical to the security of China, Japan, the Republic of Korea and, because of its alliance commitments, the United States. Its 650 million people constitute a combined economy of around US$3 trillion.

The region is vital to Australia's security, too, stretching across its northern approaches and sea lanes, the most likely approach for any military attack.

Over seventy-five years, South-East Asia has tested Australia's foreign-policy capabilities like no other part of the world. After World War II, it was where the country came to terms with the newly independent states that replaced the departing European colonial powers. A good part of Australia's diplomatic history in the second half of the twentieth century can be read as a response to the intertwined challenges of decolonisation and modernisation in the region: first the Indonesian independence struggle, then the creation of Malaysia, the Vietnam War, the Cambodian genocide and peace process, and finally the independence of Timor-Leste.

With the creation of the Association of Southeast Asian Nations (ASEAN) in 1967, bringing together Indonesia, Malaysia, the Philippines, Singapore and Thailand, then expanding to take in Brunei, the Indochina states and Myanmar, Australia had to learn how to deal effectively with regional institutions.

Over these years, Canberra had larger security stakes in Washington and London. Economically, Japan, South Korea and then China were more important. The ties of language, religion and sport were more significant in the South Pacific. But South-East Asia was where Australia had to learn to manage, mostly on its own, the politics of its neighbourhood.

These were not great powers that needed to be handled warily. Neither were they small states like those of the Pacific, which could be ignored or patronised. Like Australia, they were big enough to have a global outlook and international impact. Their actions had consequences for us.

Although, Thailand apart, they were all emerging from European colonial control, they brought to their statecraft and foreign policies centuries-long experience of responding to and absorbing the clashing interests of dynasties and empires from China in the north and India in the west, from Europe and most recently Japan. All the main religions of the world – Buddhism, Hinduism, Christianity and Islam – had passed through and left watermarks of influence.

On balance, Australia handled the challenge well. The management of Indonesia's attempts to prevent the creation of Malaysia in the 1960s – *Konfrontasi* (Confrontation) – still stands as an example of best Australian diplomatic practice. Skilfully and alone, Australian leaders sustained high-level relations with Jakarta and the mercurial President Sukarno, while making clear in words and actions their opposition to his policies. The Cambodia peace process under Gareth Evans, Peter Costello's championing of the US$1-billion Australian contributions to the IMF's financial stabilisation packages for Thailand and Indonesia during the Asian financial crisis, John Howard's generous response to the 2004 Indian Ocean tsunami, and the careful nurturing over many years of military-to-military ties all benefited our interests and built habits of cooperation.

How Canberra sidelined South-East Asia

South-East Asia is where Australia first learned the difficult lessons of managing intimate relationships with countries and cultures unlike our own. We had to balance our concern with human rights in

Suharto's Indonesia with our interest in stable economic growth and regional peace. We had to weigh our horror at the millions of deaths in the Khmer Rouge's genocide with the objective of ending further death and conflict in Cambodia.

But over recent years, South-East Asia has become less central to Australian foreign policy. The war on terrorism diverted the attention of our American ally to the Middle East, and Australia followed. Terrorism had an important regional dimension, as the Bali bombings of 2002 showed. It opened new avenues for security and intelligence cooperation. These included the Australian Federal Police's work with its Indonesian and other regional counterparts, and the Australian Defence Force's support for counterterrorism operations in the Philippines. But Australia's primary attention was on Iraq and Afghanistan.

South-East Asia was not forgotten, but by 2022 it had been sidelined

The wars in the Middle East also generated flows of refugees and asylum seekers. Often facilitated by people-smugglers, some of them transited through South-East Asia, looking for Australian sanctuary. Much else, including regional relationships, suffered as the objective of "stopping the boats" became an overriding political imperative in Canberra. "Nope, nope, nope," was Prime Minister Tony Abbott's blunt 2015 response to Indonesian and Malaysian pleas for Australia to help resettle Rohingya refugees fleeing persecution in Myanmar.

Then, after the global financial crisis in 2007–08 and Xi Jinping's elevation to leadership of the Chinese Communist Party in 2012, came another reformulation of American interests. Great-power competition, this time with China as the principal antagonist, again became the driver of US strategic policy. South-East Asia became an important arena for this competition.

Over the past five years, as the response to China became the central focus of Australian foreign policy, new priorities – the elevation of the Quad grouping, the defence partnership of AUKUS, and later the response to Russia's invasion of Ukraine – inevitably distanced it from South-East Asia. The language of Australian foreign policy changed too. The Indo-Pacific replaced the Asia-Pacific.

South-East Asia was not forgotten, but by 2022 it had been sidelined. With the Coalition cuts to the aid budget after 2014 and then a refocusing of the development assistance program on the South Pacific in an effort to preserve "our patch" from Chinese influence, Australian aid to South-East Asia declined sharply.

Despite a raft of trade agreements and the negotiation of the fifteen-nation Regional Comprehensive Economic Partnership (RCEP) agreement under ASEAN leadership, Australian trade with South-East Asian countries was sluggish, growing more slowly in the five years to 2019–20 than its trade with the European Union or the countries of APEC. Singapore (at number ten) is the only ASEAN economy to rank in Australia's top twenty destinations for overseas investment.

And while Australia has been distracted from South-East Asia, it has also become relatively less important to it. That's partly the result of the region's economic growth. In the early 1990s, Australian ministers would regularly remind their American and European colleagues that the Australian economy was larger than all the ASEAN countries combined. It is now just under one-third the size. And as the theatre of global strategic competition shifts to the Indo-Pacific, the United States, China, Japan, South Korea, India and the EU have all become more actively engaged in the battle to influence South-East Asia.

The result of these developments is that the region today feels less familiar to many Australians (apart from the 1.2 million or so South-East Asian Australians) than it did in the 1960s and '70s. The experiences of the Japanese and Vietnamese wars are fading from memory. The excitement of a period of discovery and fresh engagement with new neighbours has passed. The careers of an earlier generation of Australian journalists such as Denis Warner, Barry Wain and Graeme Dobell, who spent years living in South-East Asia and interpreting it for Australian readers, are unsustainable in the tough new media environment. Private philanthropy now supports the *Australian Financial Review*'s South-East Asia bureau.

Crucial partners

After its election in May 2022, the Albanese government declared that the goal of "deepening engagement with South-East Asia" was one of its policy priorities. Australia has a clear hierarchy of relationships with the ten ASEAN countries, though it is largely unspoken and masked by the references to "ASEAN centrality" that pepper relevant ministerial speeches. Each of the countries presents Australia with a different set of interests and histories.

Indonesia is the South-East Asian country that matters most to Australia. The reasons are obvious: the size of its population and economy, its proximity, its strategic importance, and its influence in ASEAN and the developing world. It is a key partner for Australia in the G20, APEC and the East Asia Summit.

By visiting Jakarta within two weeks of his election, Anthony Albanese continued the commendable record of all recent Australian prime ministers in engaging with the Indonesian president. The high-level rhetoric has been effusive. Former prime minister Scott Morrison declared that the two countries enjoyed a level of "trust that underpins only the truest of friendships". President Joko Widodo has visited Australia four times as president, and described Australia as Indonesia's "truest friend". We share a Comprehensive Strategic Partnership (which sounds impressive, and is a signal that the two countries take each other seriously, although it involves no irreversible commitments).

Indonesia is the largest recipient of Australian aid after Papua New Guinea (although the total amount is less than it was five years ago), and Australia's $1.56-billion loan in October 2020 provided Jakarta with much-needed budgetary support in the aftermath of the COVID-induced economic shock.

But the expressions of goodwill are not enough. The ballast Gareth Evans called for years ago to stabilise the relationship is still not bulky enough to prevent rogue waves from blowing the ship off course. Issues such as the proposal to move Australia's embassy in Israel to Jerusalem, the plans for Australian nuclear submarines, and the execution of Myuran Sukumaran and Andrew Chan for drug smuggling all agitate public opinion and disrupt official relations. Australia's responses to developments in the Indonesian provinces of Papua are a perennial source of suspicion in Jakarta. "The next bilateral spat . . . is only ever just around the corner," writes David Engel from Australian Strategic Policy Institute after years of experience as an Australian diplomat dealing with Jakarta.

Despite the massive size of the Indonesian economy and a Comprehensive Economic Partnership Agreement signed in 2020, trade and investment figures are dismally low. Indonesia ranks as Australia's thirteenth-largest trading partner, and the twenty-seventh destination for foreign investment. This reflects real difficulties for Australian businesses working in Indonesia, but plenty of other countries, including European countries with comparably sized economies such as the Netherlands, find it possible. Australian investment in Indonesia does not represent even 0.5 per cent of the total stock of Australian outwards investment.

Just 40 per cent of us agree that Indonesia is a democracy

An even more persistent problem is the level of public suspicion and ignorance on both sides. The Lowy Institute's annual public opinion survey is a sure-fire source of depression for anyone interested in relations with Indonesia. Fewer Australians trust Indonesia to act responsibly in the world than distrust it. Just 40 per cent of us agree that Indonesia is a democracy (according to a 2020 Lowy Institute poll). Australians are turning away from studying Indonesian too. The number of Bahasa Indonesia students in the final year of high school fell by 50 per cent between 2006 and 2019 to fewer than 800.

There is an equivalent drift in Indonesia. Indonesia's interests are always and understandably focused to its north. As its economy grows – and, measured by purchasing power parity, it is already larger than Australia's – Indonesia increasingly thinks of itself as in a league of its own. The Lowy Institute's 2022 poll of Indonesian public sentiment showed that just over half the respondents (55 per cent) agreed that they trusted Australia to act responsibly in the world, but this was a fall of 20 points since the last poll in 2011.

Singapore and Malaysia come next in importance to Australian interests. Old connections through the Commonwealth and people-to-people links with immigrants and students underpin the relationship. Military ties are strong, anchored in the Five Power Defence Arrangements (involving Malaysia, Singapore, Britain, Australia and New Zealand, and originally designed to reassure Singapore and Malaysia about Indonesia) and in Singapore's extensive use of Australian military training facilities. Singapore is an important source of investment in Australia.

Australia has had a long relationship with Thailand as well, a fellow American ally from the 1950s onwards. Thailand is ASEAN's second-largest economy and a top-ten trading partner for Australia. But its military-backed government and increasing closeness to China have imposed limits on the intimacy.

The relationship with Vietnam was slower to develop than others because of the war and its Communist Party government, but it has become a valuable partner. This is not just because of its millennia-long experience in dealing with China but because of the sharpness and clarity of its strategic thinking. The Vietnamese Australian community – the country's sixth-largest migrant group – matters too.

With the Philippines, the weight of the colonial and postcolonial connections with the United States, its geographic distance and the wild ride of its personality-driven domestic politics have restricted the scope of Australian engagement. But its geographic position around the South China Sea makes it strategically vital. With its worldwide diaspora it is the most extroverted of the ASEAN nations.

Larger than Thailand, Myanmar is blessed with great natural wealth but burdened by internal dissent from minority ethnic groups and controlled by the military for most of the years since it regained independence from Britain. The February 2021 coup, which snuffed out the democratic experiment led by Aung San Suu Kyi, brought international opprobrium and sparked a brutal, broad-based civil war. With its long commitment to non-interference in the internal affairs of its members, ASEAN is floundering to respond.

The nature of the emerging global competition and the permanent framework of Australia's geography will ensure that each of these political and economic relationships will be among Australia's most important in coming decades.

Understanding ASEAN

Australian policymakers and commentators sometimes talk about "ASEAN" as a collective name for the whole region, but it is also important to understand the role of the Association of Southeast Asian Nations because it is so intertwined with the way individual members think about the world and act in it.

It is easy to forget now the parlous state of regional relations in 1967 when ASEAN was formed. Indonesia's bitter political-military struggle against the creation of Malaysia had just ended. Singapore had withdrawn traumatically from the Federation of Malaysia in 1965. The Philippines pursued a claim to the Malaysian state of Sabah. Thailand, Malaysia and the Philippines were all fighting Maoist insurgencies. Indonesia had recently emerged from the bloody internal conflict in which independence leader Sukarno was replaced by General Suharto and his military-backed New Order government.

ASEAN has had many critics over the years, frustrated by its interminable meetings and formal statements so leached of meaning that all members can happily sign on. But that is to miss the point. From the beginning, ASEAN has been much less about what it can do than about what it can prevent from happening – schisms and divisions in the region and any return to inter-state conflict. For this reason, it can be difficult to recognise all that ASEAN has achieved. ASEAN's "fundamental consensus", says former Singapore diplomat Bilahari Kausikan, is always to preserve the organisation. Regional resilience is seen as strengthening national resilience.

To avoid confronting internal political tensions directly, ASEAN focused from the start on economic cooperation. Advances were slow. Despite the proclamation of an ASEAN Free Trade Area in 1992 and an ASEAN Economic Community (aiming for a single market and production base) in 2015, protectionist sentiments and demands for carve-outs have hampered any EU-style cooperation. Tariffs came down but non-tariff barriers have remained high. Robust regulatory barriers remain to cross-border flows of data and skilled workers in areas such as communications technology. Even so, progress has been made. In particular, the ASEAN-sponsored RCEP came into force in January 2022. This broad trade agreement, which also brings in China, Japan, South Korea, Australia and New Zealand, makes it easier for firms to create Asian supply chains.

The Australia–ASEAN story has been long and positive

ASEAN members also cemented their solidarity by drawing external partners into a network of ASEAN-led institutions. First came meetings with foreign officials ("Dialogues") focused on economic cooperation. Then foreign ministers became engaged. The creation of the ASEAN Regional Forum placed security issues on the agenda. In 2005, the peak organisation of the ASEAN-centred system, the East Asia Summit, was established. It would eventually expand to include China, Japan, Australia, New Zealand, South Korea, India, the United States and Russia. Finally, in 2020, the ASEAN Defence Ministers' Meeting-Plus brought defence ministers into the network. It is difficult to imagine another plausible convening mechanism for bringing together such a group. Without this network of ASEAN-cultivated institutions the Indo-Pacific region would be facing a dangerous situation in a much more vulnerable state.

The Australia–ASEAN story has been long and positive. Australia became ASEAN's first external dialogue partner in 1974, an achievement driven by the Whitlam government's efforts to expand non-military regional cooperation. Over years of solid diplomatic work, Australia helped empower the association's secretariat through its aid program, established a resident mission to ASEAN in Jakarta in 2013, and supported the development of its institutions. It was a founding member of the East Asia Summit. Most recently, in 2020, ASEAN agreed to annual leaders' meetings with Australia, and these were reinforced with the establishment of a Comprehensive Strategic Partnership in 2021. Whenever ASEAN members saw Australia's eyes straying, they pounced quickly, smothering at birth Kevin Rudd's 2008 proposals for a broader "Asia-Pacific Community", for example.

Despite the many pressures it faces, including China–US competition, internal conflict in Myanmar and, currently, the COVID-19 pandemic, ASEAN is likely to survive because it remains useful to all its members. It helps them shelter behind a coordinated ASEAN consensus and avoid unwanted choices. It suits Australia too, buttressing our interest in keeping the region together in a world of decoupling and deconstruction.

From time to time the suggestion is made that Australia should join ASEAN. For their reasons and ours, that is unlikely. It is already difficult enough for current members to manage agreement on difficult issues without adding Australia and our alliance complications into the mix. And, to be honest, we would drive each other crazy. The ASEAN way – low-keyed, allusive, indirect – is not Australia's.

Challenges of great-power rivalry

The next decade will be more challenging for the ASEAN states. South-East Asia benefited from globalisation more than any other part of the world, except perhaps China. The region's combined GDP more than doubled in the past twenty years as it plugged its industries into global supply chains. Its cities grew. With good use of digital innovations, and a sophisticated online market for goods and services, middle-class consumers increased in number.

But as supply chains are reconfigured in response to security concerns, and a more divided world economy emerges, ASEAN's development model will be tested. The hurdle of the "middle-income trap" lies ahead for all the large ASEAN members. This term, devised by the World Bank, describes the problem faced by countries which want to move beyond export-driven, low-cost manufacturing but must make a grand leap to productivity-boosting innovation if they are to get there.

At the same time, and another barrier to this objective, the political systems in Myanmar, Thailand, the Philippines and Malaysia are all under stress, and it is possible that the high point of Indonesian democracy has passed.

Geopolitically and geoeconomically, the South-East Asian states will be pressed to take sides in a great-power competition they would much rather avoid. Some ASEAN members are American allies. Some like Cambodia, are close to China. But all of them have a deep interest in China's capacity through markets, investment and expertise to contribute to their development, while avoiding Beijing's control and keeping the region conflict-free.

The desire to keep outside powers from direct confrontation in the region long predates the latest round of China–US competition. ASEAN's 1971 declaration of South-East Asia as a Zone of Peace, Freedom and Neutrality (ZOPFAN) committed members to a region "free of any form or manner of interference by outside powers". This loose norm of non-alignment is now embedded deeply.

Even Singapore, perpetually alert to shifts in the global balance, and more willing than its partners to provide support to the United States, is a long way from providing full-throated support for one side in a binary world. As Prime Minister Lee Hsien Loong explained to Scott Morrison at a press conference in June 2021:

> The relationship with China is one of the biggest foreign policy quesions for every major power in the world. You will need to work with the country – it is going to be there, it is going to be a substantial presence, and you can cooperate with it, you can engage it, you can negotiate with it but it has to be a long and mutually constructive process. You do not have to become like them, neither can you hope to make them become like you.

In the words of the Indonesian scholar Evan Laksmana: "In Asia, hierarchy, rather than power balance, has historically been the structure of regional order ... Regional countries will continue ... engaging both sides and hedging their bets. They will choose the options that enhance their domestic legitimacy and strategic autonomy."

The values of Western liberalism cannot be the basis for Australia's engagement with South-East Asia

So if Australia's primary strategic objective in South-East Asia is to build coalitions against China, it will be disappointed. ASEAN announced a Comprehensive Strategic Partnership with China just days after signing a similar agreement with Australia. And if the countries of the region judge that Australia has no independent ability to interact with Beijing, it will be less relevant to them.

What can the basis of Australia's relationship with South-East

Asia be in this period of change? Our goals are clear. We want a region that remains free of tension (thereby keeping it away from Australia). We want independent neighbours who are not vulnerable to external coercion. We want an integrated, prosperous regional economy, open to Australian trade and investment. We want partners who share our interests in a predictable world order in which rules governing trade, communications, the global environment, health and warfare are mutually negotiated and consistently followed.

A new Australian statecraft

After Australian forces withdrew from the Middle East and the war on terrorism ratcheted down, the language of Australian foreign policy became simpler and more binary. The central element of the world order was portrayed as a confrontation between democracies and an "arc of autocracies". With the Ukraine war, terms like "the West" and "the Free World", last heard widely during the Cold War have become part of common rhetoric again.

But the values of Western liberalism cannot be the basis for Australia's engagement with South-East Asia. None of the states of the region identifies as a liberal democracy and there is not much point in talking to Indonesia or Thailand as fellow members of "the West". According to the Economist Intelligence Unit's annual Democracy Index, all the ASEAN states lie somewhere on a spectrum between "Flawed Democracies" and "Authoritarian States". Vietnam is run by a Communist Party just as committed to preserving the monopoly of power as its Chinese counterpart. Brunei is an autocracy under the control of a hereditary monarch.

That means Australia must find an inclusive foreign-policy language that deepens our conversations with our neighbours. This does not require us to deny the values of our democratic system or the realities of our US alliance. As former Department of Foreign Affairs and Trade secretary Peter Varghese puts it: "[Values] should define who we are, not what we insist others become."

Richard Maude, from the Asia Society Policy Institute, and chief drafter of Australia's 2017 Foreign Policy White Paper, makes the important suggestion that Australia's focus should be "less on shared values and more on 'shared principles'". Such principles might include respect for national sovereignty, the peaceful settlement of disputes, the non-use of coercion, and respect for international law, especially in the UN Convention on the Law of the Sea. Identifying shared interests and principles and aligning them with our values is the starting point for the work of engaging with South-East Asia.

In the toolbox of statecraft there are broadly three ways to apply influence on other countries. You can use *inducement* to buy an outcome, you can apply *coercion* to force it, or you can *persuade* the other side by force of argument and appeals to mutual interests. In South-East Asia, Australia is not rich or powerful enough to utilise the first two. That leaves us with the task of persuasion.

The first requirement is to understand South-East Asia. How can we persuade our neighbours unless we know what is persuasive to them? Australia needs to be able to draw upon a strong body of diplomats, officials and military officers who know the various countries of South-East Asia, speak their languages and have developed relationships over time with its decision-makers. That goes for our political leaders as well. We need more politicians whose WhatsApp and Signal contact lists span the region, and they need to be encouraged to keep turning up in South-East Asian capitals. As Susannah Patton from the Lowy Institute has pointed out, it has been twenty years and more since the last bilateral visits by Australian prime ministers to Thailand and the Philippines.

Backing up such frontline operational expertise, Australia also must ensure that the foundational research and analytical capabilities of our universities and think tanks are the best in the world at dealing with South-East Asia. We need to teach its history, languages and cultures, modern as well as ancient. That requires continued investment.

The second requirement is to accept that our ability to persuade regional governments and shape outcomes requires Australia to engage them on issues of importance to them, not just us. For all the ASEAN states, development remains a primary goal. According to the Asian Development Bank, 24 million people in South-East Asia were still subsisting on less than US$1.90 a day in 2021.

Areas on which we can cooperate (and already are cooperating) include climate change, health, renewable energy, and vocational and technical education. Most of the large South-East Asian economies have moved beyond the sort of development assistance traditionally delivered by the Australia aid program. Our new challenge is to find ways of investing in economic partnerships with ASEAN countries in areas such as these that will help us to align our national development objectives and the standards and systems that underpin them.

The hard work of underpinning our economic relationships with stronger trade and investment ties is not something governments themselves can achieve. Exporters, importers and investors have to make their own decisions. But as we can see from the fact that Australia has more direct investment in New Zealand than in all ten ASEAN states combined, familiarity and ease of operation are major issues for the business community. Government support, and even handholding, is essential. A good example of what might be done is the Morrison government's support for Katalis (Catalyst), a bi-national, business-supported enterprise designed to identify trade and investment opportunities arising from the Indonesia-Australia Comprehensive Economic Partnership Agreement.

South-East Asia . . . will be the place Australian foreign policy can influence outcomes more consequentially than anywhere else

The Australian Defence Force's multigenerational efforts to develop personal and professional relationships with its ASEAN counterparts have paid dividends many times over, as any Australian ambassador in the region will acknowledge. Cooperative programs and exercises are sustained by the Department of Defence in areas from humanitarian and disaster relief to cyber security.

In the twenty-first century, however, Australia's defence focus has been overwhelmingly on support for and from the US alliance, and more recently on the Five Eyes partnership and AUKUS. To deal most effectively with South-East Asia, Australia must be willing to step beyond its comfort zone. Paul Keating's 1996 Agreement on Maintaining Security with Indonesia stands, in its objectives and language, as an example of how Australia might reinforce defence relationships with regional countries, by focusing on our mutual needs to maintain an autonomous security capability in the region rather than on geostrategic competition. That agreement was a victim of the bilateral strains during the East Timor independence struggle, but it was supported by both sides of Australian politics when it was announced.

In a hard world of military rivalry and conflict, the phrase "people-to-people relations" sounds trifling. But as the experience of the Australian Defence Force shows, investment in networks and contacts pays valuable practical dividends. Many of Indonesia's most eminent economists and economic decision-makers have obtained their PhDs through a decades-long effort by the Australian National University's Indonesia Project to build academic links. Working in the other direction, projects like the New Colombo Plan are helping young Australians experience South-East Asia and build ties with a new generation of its leaders. Whatever the area, from music to farming, deeper community links will be a long-lasting asset for Australia, helping to shape common understandings of our future.

A final requirement is to have the architecture in place to enable us to engage effectively with the region. Thanks to the good work of different governments over many decades, Australia has a head start here. With our main partners, and with ASEAN as an institution, we have regular, well-tested forums and processes at officials', ministerial and prime ministerial levels. If Australia has the ideas, the opportunities to take them forward are there.

A new international order will emerge from the current turmoil, but its elements might be unclear for years. Its shape will depend primarily on whether the US can resolve its internal political divisions and carry forward a grand strategy that is both principled and consistent through changing administrations, and whether China concludes that its interests are best served by working cooperatively within a comprehensive global system.

South-East Asia, Australia's near abroad, will never present us with easy options. But it will be the place Australian foreign policy can influence outcomes more consequentially than anywhere else in the world, including the South Pacific. The way our policymakers shape and manage these relationships, and their success or failure in working with regional partners to fashion purposeful and coherent responses to unprecedented global challenges, will be the great test of Australian foreign policy in the challenging times ahead. ■

RED FLAGS

China's expanding footprint in South-East Asia

Sebastian Strangio

On a humid morning in early December, a group of suited dignitaries gathered on the platform of a recently completed train station in Vientiane, the capital of Laos. A scrum of press photographers rattled away as the officials, most of them from Laos and China, filed past a row of Buddhist monks seated on a dais under a large billboard that featured an image of two Chinese-made bullet trains, painted in the colours of the Lao national flag: red, white and blue.

The ceremony was held to inaugurate a new high-speed railway line connecting Vientiane to the southern Chinese city of Kunming, some 1035 kilometres to the north. After the officials made offerings to the monks, Lao prime minister Phankham Viphavanh lit sticks of incense at a nearby shrine and struck a brass gong nine times, symbolising the nine virtues of the Buddha. The monks then sprinkled blessed water against the flank of one of the snub-nosed Lane Xang electric multiple unit (EMU) locomotives – named after the precolonial kingdom which once ruled much of the expanse of modern Laos – that had recently rolled down the line from China.

The inauguration of the Laos–China railway, which began construction in late 2016, was a milestone for the communist government of Laos, which had long harboured a desire to break out of its rugged, landlocked geography. For most of history, the 417 kilometres dividing Vientiane and the Chinese border would have taken weeks, if not months, to traverse; as recently as last decade, it required a two-day trip on serpentine, pot-holed roads. The Lane Xang EMUs had cut travel times to a mere four hours. Prime Minister Phankham, speaking on board the train during its inaugural trip northwards, told state media that the US$5.9 billion project was "conducive to the economic and social development of Laos" and would help advance the government's strategy of "transforming Laos from a land-locked country to a land-linked country".

While the railway's passenger services have a top speed of 160 kilometres per hour, far slower than most high-speed rail systems, the line is nonetheless a striking instance of Chinese technical prowess. Given the rugged terrain, the Lao segment of the railway required the construction of 198 kilometres of tunnels and 61 kilometres of bridges: hence, its considerable cost. As the first international extension of China's own high-speed rail network, the Laos–China Railway was a landmark achievement of Chinese president Xi Jinping's headline Belt and Road Initiative (BRI) infrastructure scheme. It was also the first step in the fulfilment of an old European imperial dream: the linking of China to Singapore by rail.

For Laos, a communist-ruled nation of 7 million, the railway's completion in the last few months of 2021 had little historical precedent. Despite today sharing a short border with the People's Republic of China, the country's rough terrain had long shielded it from the influence of the succession of dynasties and empires that held sway over the cradle of Chinese civilisation in the Yellow River basin. To be sure, Chinese chroniclers claimed the kingdom of Lane Xang as a vassal state from the late fourteenth century, but in practice it existed at the outer rim of imperial concerns, "secluded at the edge of the sky", as the Yongzheng Emperor opined in the eighteenth century. The terrain also inhibited Chinese immigration to Laos on the scale that took place to other parts of South-East Asia – to British Malaya, the Dutch East Indies, French Indochina and the Kingdom of Siam – in the late nineteenth and early twentieth centuries. By 1960, just 30,000 ethnic Chinese resided in Laos, compared with an estimated 350,000 in Cambodia and 800,000 in South Vietnam.

By the time of the railway's launch on 2 December – the forty-sixth anniversary of the takeover of Laos by the communist Pathet Lao – this cloistered world was a distant memory. Two decades of infrastructure development had breached the thick barrier of mountains and forests that once kept Chinese power and influence at arm's length. This had drawn in a wave of enterprising Chinese expatriates, along with flows of Chinese capital that have developed mining operations, hydropower dams, industrial-scale agricultural plantations and skyline-altering real estate developments. Greased by intimate relations with Laos's venal political and commercial elite, Chinese influence now rivals that of the nation's fraternal bosom buddy wartime ally, Vietnam.

This wave of investment and emigration from China has profoundly altered the physical landscape of northern Laos. In quiet provincial capitals such as Udomxai and Luang Namtha, both of which have stations on the new railway line, Chinese nationals now make up as much as a fifth of the population and the streets are dotted with Chinese-run restaurants, hotels, vehicle repair shops and furniture stores. Prior to the COVID-19 pandemic, Chinese nationals also represented the largest proportion of tourists to Laos, and cars bearing Chinese licence plates had become a common sight on the streets of Luang Prabang, the graceful former royal capital nestled in a verdant bend of the Mekong river. While outbound Chinese tourism remains dammed up for now behind Beijing's strict "zero COVID" policy, the long-term impact of the Laos–China Railway will be to further this process of economic integration and bind these two neighbours more tightly together than ever before.

For China, proximity makes South-East Asia a region of crucial importance

China's gateway to the world

The transformation of Laos reflects in miniature the impact that China's rising power is having on South-East Asia. Like Laos, the mainland South-East Asian nations that are territorially contiguous with China – Myanmar, Thailand, Cambodia and Vietnam – have witnessed the profound impacts of integrative infrastructure projects. This network of highways, bridges, river ports and special economic zones, initiated under Japanese auspices in the 1990s but now spearheaded overwhelmingly by Beijing, have supercharged the mule-trading routes and opium-smuggling trails that once wound through the hills. In so doing, they have slowly reoriented the Mekong region's economic centre of gravity, shifting it from southern port cities such as Bangkok and Yangon – long its primary gateways to the global economy – towards the north, and opening the Mekong region to a transformative southward sweep of Chinese investment and immigration.

Parallel developments have taken place in the maritime region of South-East Asia, which is home to the nations of Malaysia, Singapore, Indonesia, Brunei, the Philippines and Timor-Leste. Since the 1980s, China has built a powerful navy to secure the sea lanes on which the Chinese economy relies. In the South China Sea, which laps the shores of eight South-East Asian nations, Beijing has asserted this newfound naval power, menacing fishing vessels operating within its audacious "nine-dash line", which lops off large swathes of ocean claimed by Malaysia, Vietnam, Brunei and the Philippines. As on the mainland, flows of Chinese capital and mammoth infrastructure projects – in this case, the construction of island fortresses on low-tide elevations and specks of coral in disputed parts of the seaway – have collapsed the distance that once separated China from the peoples and states of archipelagic South-East Asia.

These developments are in many ways a logical outgrowth of China's remarkable economic renaissance. In 1992, China's per capita GDP sat at just US$366, and the value of its exports amounted to less than $67 billion, according to the World Bank; by 2020, its per capita GDP had grown by twenty-eight times, while its exports had increased forty-fold. They also reflect the confidence and ambition that China's boom has engendered. Shortly after ascending to the apex of the Chinese party-state in November 2012, Xi Jinping vowed to restore China to its ancient prominence, speaking of the "great rejuvenation of the Chinese nation". He has since consolidated his control at home, reinforcing the position of the Chinese Communist Party (CCP) at the nucleus of the nation's political and economic life, while becoming more assertive abroad, pressing controversial claims in the South and East China seas and taking a more pugnacious approach to relations with the West. In essence, Xi's goal is the same as that of past generations of Chinese leaders and reformers: to build up his nation's wealth and power, expunge its "century of humiliation" at the hands of the Western empires and imperial Japan, and restore China to its former status as the pre-eminent power in Asia.

For China, proximity makes South-East Asia a region of crucial importance. The region is home to a young and growing population of

650 million, and the ten nations of the Association of Southeast Asian Nations (ASEAN) have a collective economy of $2.8 trillion, smaller only than the economies of the United States, China, the European Union, Japan and India. Perhaps more importantly, South-East Asia straddles the sea lanes that form the connective tissue of China's export-focused economy. As China's economy expanded in the 1980s, its growing export of manufactured products to world markets and its increasing reliance on crude oil from the Middle East highlighted its paralysing reliance on the narrow Straits of Malacca, which lie between peninsular Malaysia and the Indonesian island of Sumatra and offer the most direct link between the Pacific and Indian oceans. This "Malacca dilemma", as Chinese president Hu Jintao referred to it in 2003, spurred the modernisation of the Chinese navy and provides a strategic rationale for China's maximalist claims in the South China Sea. It also shaped China's integration with mainland South-East Asia: increasing overland connectivity has given China direct access to the Indian Ocean, while helping to accelerate the development of China's poverty-stricken and landlocked south-west provinces.

For a Chinese establishment that sees its nation ringed by potential rivals, from nuclear-armed Russia and India to the string of US allies and partners – Japan, South Korea, Taiwan and the Philippines – lying off its eastern seaboard, South-East Asia appears relatively receptive to the spread of Chinese influence. Despite the US treaty alliances with Thailand and the Philippines, the region is not home to a predominant great power, and the presence in most countries of large and prosperous ethnic Chinese diaspora communities, some of them centuries old, has created fertile conditions for economic interaction. According to Marvin Ott, a senior fellow at the Foreign Policy Research Institute in Washington DC, South-East Asia figures as "a southern portico" for China, "a potential bridge between interior/southern China and the tropical seas along the equator". It is no exaggeration to state that Xi's road to national rejuvenation runs directly through the ocean straits and mountain passes of South-East Asia.

Stoking fears and memories

The same features that make South-East Asia crucial to Chinese strategists make it important for those powers, such as the United States, Japan, India and Australia, collectively known as the "Quad", that are seeking to contain China's growing power and ambition. Under President Donald Trump, US attitudes and policy towards China took a sharp negative turn – one that has largely persisted under Joe Biden. Where earlier US administrations saw Beijing as both a competitor and potential partner, and dreamed of turning it into a "responsible stakeholder" in a US-led international system, recent American policy documents have depicted it as an unqualified adversary and a fundamental threat to US interests. A bipartisan consensus now holds that

South-East Asian views of China are more complex and anguished

China is a predatory power that bullies its neighbours, seeks to export its authoritarian political model and employs "debt-trap diplomacy" to ensnare developing nations. Similar views have migrated to Australia, sharpening in the aftermath of China's restrictions of Australian imports in 2020. In September 2021, defence minister Peter Dutton said that China had become "increasingly bellicose" and that its activities were "increasingly coercive, driven by a zero-sum mentality".

In Washington and Canberra (though less so in New Delhi), this malign image is typically set against an idealised vision of American primacy and the US-led "rules-based order" that China is allegedly working to supplant. Since Biden's inauguration, several high-level US officials, including Vice President Kamala Harris, Secretary of State Antony Blinken and Secretary of Defence Lloyd Austin, have carried this message to South-East Asian capitals, pledging closer ties and contrasting its vision for a "free and open Indo-Pacific" with China's repressive conception of regional and global order. The US Navy continues to mount freedom of navigation operations, or FONOPs, through the South China Sea, and through the establishment of the Mekong–US Partnership in 2020, Washington has dialled up its warnings about the deleterious social and ecological impact of China's cascade of dams on the headwaters of the Mekong River. South-East Asia – perhaps the quintessential "Indo-Pacific" region – has once again become the object of intensifying superpower competition.

While Western pundits and politicians have become fond of framing this competition as a struggle between "democracy" and "authoritarianism", or between a "free world" and a malign "arc of autocracy", as Prime Minister Scott Morrison put it in March 2022, South-East Asian views of China are more complex and anguished. This reflects the Janus-faced quality of geographic proximity, which makes China both an object of concern and a reality that no nation can ignore. In 1971, three years before his government established relations with Mao's China, Malaysia's then prime minister, Tun Abdul Razak, observed that South-East Asia's proximity to China meant that it would always be "the first to live with the consequences of her policies".

This has been both bane and blessing. During the Cold War, South-East Asia was for the Chinese leader Mao Zedong a vale of revolutionary experimentation that involved moral and material support for communist insurgencies from Vietnam to Kalimantan. As China pivoted from Mao's fiery ideological insurrectionism to the economic pragmatism of Deng Xiaoping in the 1980s, the region became a focus of Chinese economic engagement: diplomatic relations blossomed as Cold War tensions thawed and trade between the two started to surge, enabled in part by a reawakening of commercial and cultural ties between the ethnic Chinese business communities in Southeast Asia and their ancestral homeland.

Over the past fifteen years, as China's power has grown and it has become more assertive, particularly in the South China Sea, memories of Chinese subversion have resurfaced. This includes both its support for communist insurgencies and the related question of its relationship with ethnic Chinese communities, a fear rooted in the rise of

Chinese nationalism in the late nineteenth and early twentieth centuries, and its subsequent spread to ethnic Chinese communities abroad.

These echoes have been amplified by the negative impacts of China's increasing influence. In many parts of South-East Asia, large-scale infrastructure developments have, as in China, swept people off their land and caused serious social and environmental harm. For instance, in Myanmar, widespread public opposition to the Chinese-backed Myitsone hydropower dam in the northern state of Kachin, which would have flooded an area the size of Singapore and exported most of the power produced to nearby Yunnan province, helped prod the country's military towards a significant, if ultimately failed, project of political and economic opening in the 2010s.

Another negative impact has been growing debt. While the meme of "debt-trap diplomacy" – Beijing's alleged intention to entrap small developing nations in skeins of debt – has been convincingly debunked by scholars, there is no doubt that debt poses real risks, which have often stoked elite and public angst. During visits to Malaysia in late 2017, I heard many people express concerns about the weight of debt that the government of then prime minister Najib Razak had taken on in large-scale Belt and Road Initiative (BRI) deals with China. Similar concerns were aired in Myanmar after Aung San Suu Kyi's National League for Democracy (NLD) took power in 2016, inheriting a slew of major deals signed during the years of military rule. For Laos, the immense cost of the Laos–China Railway – the nation's total liability from the project sits at around US$1.54 billion – burdened it with heavy debt, even before the COVID-19 pandemic sent the country into recession. In September 2020, swamped by rising debt, Laos announced that it was ceding majority control of its national power grid to a majority Chinese-owned joint venture.

China has done little to assuage these various fears. Indeed, its behaviour has achieved the opposite. China's return to great power status has been accompanied by an assumption that South-East Asian states should defer to its wishes. Meanwhile, Beijing has not hesitated to employ its economic power for political and strategic ends, such as when it cut off imports of tropical fruit from the Philippines, in response to the two nations' 2012 stand-off over the Scarborough Shoal in the South China Sea. This imperious attitude was on display during the 17th ASEAN Regional Forum in the Vietnamese capital, Hanoi, in July 2010, when Yang Jiechi, then minister of foreign affairs, declared that maritime disputes between China and ASEAN member states in the South China Sea would not be negotiated multilaterally. "China is a big country and other countries are small countries," he reportedly told South-East Asian leaders, "and that's just a fact."

China's increased outreach risks reawakening old fears of dual loyalties

While Beijing is adept at red-carpet pageantry and state-level diplomacy, its officials have difficulty engaging with the region's more open societies, and with any constituencies lying beyond the remit of the state. This has contributed to Beijing's inability to respond effectively to the negative reactions to its rise, and even to grasp that its actions could arouse such reactions in the first place.

This was made clear in the aftermath of the Myanmar armed forces' coup in February 2021, when China became the subject of fierce public anger for its rumoured support for the military. In the weeks after the takeover, as mass protests roiled the streets, demonstrators gathered outside the Chinese embassy in Yangon. Later, during a violent crackdown in the city's industrial Hlaingthaya district, protesters smashed, looted and vandalised thirty-two Chinese-financed factories, in retaliation for China's perceived support for the military government. Beijing evinced little understanding as to how or why its policies had angered the public. While the Chinese embassy called on the regime to "ensure the safety of life and property of Chinese companies and personnel in Myanmar", the *Global Times* deflected blame elsewhere, airing the possibility that those suspected of damaging Chinese factories were "anti-China locals who have been provoked by some Western anti-China forces, NGOs, and Hong Kong secessionists". It made similar allegations about the protests against the Myitsone dam in 2011.

Beijing's most dangerous misstep involves its recent attempts to broaden its outreach to the ethnic Chinese populations of South-East Asia. As the Indonesian scholar Leo Suryadinata notes, Xi's China has made increasing references to Overseas Chinese as part of a "great Chinese family", and sought to convert the ethnic affiliations and business connections of South-East Asian Chinese into support for Chinese strategic initiatives such as the BRI. This remains one of the most sensitive aspects of China's growing influence in the region, one that threatens to blur an important line between Chinese nationality and ethnicity. In countries such as Indonesia and Malaysia, where ethnic Chinese have historically been subject to discrimination and violent attacks, most recently in Indonesia in 1998, this distinction has been crucial to the acceptance of ethnic Chinese as members of the national community. China's increased outreach risks reawakening old fears of dual loyalties.

The region's consternation about China's growing power was reflected in a survey of South-East Asian regional experts and policymakers released in early 2022 by the ISEAS–Yusof Ishak Institute in Singapore. Fifty-eight per cent of respondents expressed either "little confidence" (33 per cent) or "no confidence" (25 per cent) in China to "do the right thing" to contribute to global peace, security, prosperity and governance. Of those who were distrustful of China, 50 per cent expressed fear that it could use its economic and military power to threaten their nation's interests and sovereignty. Nearly a quarter said that they did not consider China "a responsible or reliable power".

Wary of the West

To counterbalance China's growing strategic weight, most South-East Asian governments strongly desire improved economic and security relations with the United States and other prominent powers, including Japan, Australia, South Korea, Russia and the European Union. At the same time, most are reluctant to sign up to any coalition aimed, implicitly or otherwise, at containing China or curbing its influence. For all their concerns, proximity gives South-East Asian governments a strong stake in China's continued stability and prosperity. As many in the region recall, periods of instability or civil war within China have historically produced destabilising flows of people southwards. The fall of the Ming dynasty in the seventeenth century led to an exodus of refugees into South-East Asia, as did the colossal internal rebellions of the late Qing dynasty and, most recently, the collapse of nationalist China to the communists in 1949. South-East Asian governments have similarly few yearnings for the China of Mao, which cut itself off from normal commercial intercourse and actively sought the armed overthrow of Southeast Asian governments.

Consternation about China's rising power is tempered by the reality that it is now central to South-East Asia's future prosperity. China is the leading trading partner of eight of the ten ASEAN countries. From 2013 to 2018, China's trade with the South-East Asian bloc totalled $2.37 trillion, compared to $1.33 trillion for the United States and $1.32 trillion for Japan. Chinese investment flows into ASEAN have increased at a slower rate, but by 2018, five years after the launch of the BRI, China had become the second-largest investor in ASEAN from outside the region, behind Japan. From Mandalay to Singapore, China's banks, energy companies, tech firms and real-estate conglomerates are an increasingly visible, and indispensable, presence;

so too are its students, tourists and businesspeople. China's economic centrality is only cast into relief by Washington's retreat from ambitious multilateral trade deals following Trump's withdrawal from the Trans-Pacific Partnership trade pact in early 2017. Even under Biden, economics remains the gaping hole at the centre of the US government's Indo-Pacific strategy.

This reality has been underscored since the onset of the COVID-19 pandemic. Chinese foreign minister Wang Yi has visited every ASEAN nation since the beginning of the pandemic, pledging shipments of vaccines and presenting China as a necessary partner in their efforts to beat back the coronavirus and haul their economies out of recession. As of June 2021, South-East Asia had accounted for 29 per cent of China's total vaccine donations and 26 per cent of its worldwide vaccine sales. In November, Xi pledged an additional 150 million doses for the ASEAN bloc.

The ten ASEAN nations differ considerably on the question of China

While Western observers have pointed out the relatively poor efficacy of China's Sinovac and Sinopharm vaccines – a fact that is not lost on South-East Asian publics, who have jostled to obtain the mRNA vaccines produced by the US firms Pfizer and Moderna – rich-world vaccine hoarding means that most South-East Asian nations have had no real alternatives. Chinese vaccines have been pivotal in Indonesia's ambitious drive to vaccinate its 273 million people, and to

Cambodia achieving an impressive 83 per cent two-dose vaccination rate by April of this year. Indonesian foreign minister Retno Marsudi in particular has been vocal about the "deep inequality" of the global COVID-19 response, describing equal access to vaccines as the "biggest moral test before the global community".

While South-East Asian governments view China with some ambivalence, they are also ambivalent about the United States and the "rules-based order" that it claims to represent. Partly this is because many South-East Asian leaders remember well, in some cases personally, what the extension of this order to South-East Asia involved: namely, the long and destructive American intervention in Vietnam, Cambodia and Laos, and sustained US support for a line of venal strongmen autocrats, including the Philippines' Ferdinand Marcos and Indonesia's General Suharto, as well as support for the latter's massacre of up to a million suspected communists in 1965–66. To drive home this point after the opening of the Laos–China Railway in December, Hu Xijin, the combative former editor-in-chief of the *Global Times*, posted an image on Twitter juxtaposing its completion with the US Air Force's carpet bombing of Laos during the Vietnam War. The region, like China, has benefited greatly from the US-backed security order, but it neither idealises US power nor views American behaviour as fundamentally more peaceful or consensual than that of China.

Partly, too, it reflects the profound experience of Western imperialism. The region's bruising encounter with the Western empires, and later imperial Japan, which in places like Vietnam and Indonesia ultimately involved a bloody struggle for national self-determination, inculcated a profound commitment to the norm of state sovereignty and an abiding scepticism about Western universalist claims. After the end of the Cold War, South-East Asian leaders, including Singapore's Lee Kuan Yew and Malaysia's Mahathir Mohamad, were prominent in the "Asian values" debates that sought to push back against the liberal triumphalism that followed the collapse of the Soviet Union. China's promotion of an international order based on a reassertion of the norm of sovereignty – however strained and contradicted by its fence-sitting over Russia's invasion of Ukraine – thus represents an important area of overlapping interest with South-East Asian governments.

This tendency has produced a persistent pattern in regional diplomacy, one that almost approaches an iron law: where Western nations have pressured or criticised South-East Asian governments over democratic backsliding or human rights issues, they have tended to turn to China for diplomatic backing and "no-strings" financial support. The cardinal example is Cambodia's prime minister, Hun Sen, who over the past three decades has steered his country into a close alignment with Beijing, as a shield against the democratising energies unleashed by a United Nations peacekeeping mission that was dispatched to Cambodia at the end of the Cold War. Even for leaders less beholden to Beijing than Hun Sen, China's pragmatic form of "non-interference", and its avowed respect for each nation's right "to choose its own development path", has been greatly appreciated, even as China's own behaviour takes on echoes of imperial powers past.

Where empires collide

In today's South-East Asia, the desire for mutually beneficial economic relations with China, and the fear of its expanding power, coexist and comingle, feeding back and forth in a constant blur of iterations. While this essay has focused, at the risk of some oversimplification, on the common threads among the eleven nations of South-East Asia, each has perceived and responded to the China challenge in different ways. The equation is very different for Vietnam, which sits in particularly close geographic and cultural proximity to China, than for archipelagic Indonesia, where views of China are filtered through perceptions of the waves of immigrants that have alighted on its shores since the midpoint of the last millennium. Some nations have proven adept at incorporating China into a balanced diet of foreign relations, while others, such as communist-ruled Laos and Cambodia under Hun Sen, have allowed themselves to sleepwalk into a blithe overreliance on China's easy money and "no-strings" approach to governance. Each nation's particular approach to China reflects both its geographic orientation vis-a-vis China and its long history of interaction with the Chinese state and the South-East Asians who once called China home.

However, growing competition between China and the United States and its partners is placing additional strain on South-East Asia's ability to maintain its strategic autonomy. This is true both at the national level and within ASEAN. Established in 1967 at the height of the Cold War, ASEAN's purpose was to create a mechanism by which the small nations of the region could preserve some measure of autonomy in the midst of great-power competition. In the early 1970s, facing the US drawdown from Vietnam and the withdrawal of British forces from East of Suez, Singapore's first foreign minister, S. Rajaratnam, observed that South-East Asia "must fill what some people call the power vacuum itself or resign itself to the dismal prospect of the vacuum being filled from outside".

For the duration of the Cold War, it served this purpose with some success. The most convincing evidence of this was not simply that ASEAN headed off conflict between its five founding members, but that it successfully constrained and incorporated the region's most populous and potentially hegemonic state: Indonesia.

South-East Asians are no strangers to strategic turbulence

Since the end of the Cold War, however, ASEAN's development has presented a paradox. In the 1990s, it expanded its membership to include four nations in close proximity to China – military-ruled Myanmar and the communist (or formerly communist) nations of Vietnam, Cambodia and Laos – aligning ASEAN with the generally recognised boundaries of South-East Asia. (It also admitted Timor-Leste, which gained independence from Indonesia in 2002.) But even as "ASEAN" has grown to become a synonym for "South-East Asia", the bloc's increased political diversity has made it trickier to agree on key issues. Currently, the ten ASEAN nations differ considerably on the question of China, and, in particular, on the South China Sea disputes.

Given the bloc's consensus-based decision-making, Beijing has been able to drive wedges of economic inducement between member states, most recently at an ASEAN foreign ministers' meeting in 2012, when Cambodia intervened to veto mild criticisms of China's actions in the South China Sea. Growing US–China tensions could eventually begin to weaken South-East Asian unity. This is all the riskier given that many South-East Asian governments are preoccupied by other concerns, from simple elite self-preservation and economic recovery to simmering ethnic conflict and insurgency – the unfinished business of nation-building in the shadow of empire.

At the same time, South-East Asians are no strangers to strategic turbulence. Major powers have often collided in the region. Starting in the sixteenth century, South-East Asia was conquered and carved up by the Portuguese, British, Dutch, Spanish, French and Americans, who frequently clashed in their pursuit of the region's riches. Later, the Cold War burned hotter there than just about anywhere else. This experience has inculcated a congenital desire to balance between the competing poles of international power. Thailand cherishes its ability to bend hither and thither, like "bamboo in the wind". Indonesians speak of "rowing between two reefs". Vietnam nurtures its own brand of "bamboo diplomacy".

Bilahari Kausikan, the former permanent secretary of Singapore's Ministry of Foreign Affairs, has written that South-East Asian diplomacy is instinctively "promiscuous, not monogamous" and seeks "to hedge, balance, and bandwagon simultaneously". The era of unipolar

American hegemony, he wrote, has largely given way to a multi-polar world that "facilitates this instinct because it maximises room for manoeuvre and the exercise of agency". In a new era of superpower competition that is likely to be prolonged, with no clear denouement, the prosperity and security of the South-East Asian nations will hinge on how successfully they are able to draw on this heritage: to dance and weave, and muddle their way through the reefs and shoals of a tenser, more constrained world. ■

STRONGMEN INC.

The Marcos comeback

Nicole Curato

1.

The Marcoses are back in power. Thirty-six years after dictator Ferdinand Marcos was ousted by a popular uprising, his son and namesake was elected the seventeenth president of the Republic of the Philippines. He won in a landslide.

Two days after the polls closed, Ferdinand "Bongbong" Marcos Jr was photographed carrying a placard that read "Thank you 31 Million", referring to the number of votes he received, as he greeted his supporters in his campaign headquarters in Manila. "The people spoke decisively," his statement read. He promised to "seek common ground across political divides".

For some observers, the political comeback of the Marcoses signals the end of liberal democracy in the Philippines. The country that Václav Havel considered an inspiration for the wave of velvet revolutions in

Eastern Europe now tells the world that the revolution was not worth it. Memes and TikTok videos portray the Marcos years as the golden age of the Philippines. Bridges were built, schoolchildren were fed, the people were disciplined – the Philippines was the envy of the world. Erased from these stories are the thousands disappeared, detained and killed, as well as the billions of dollars the Marcos family plundered from the nation. Marcos Jr urged the nation not to dwell on the past but instead look to the future. That the Philippines will rise again was his campaign promise.

The question is: how, precisely, will the country rise again? The Philippines is illustrative of the broader trend of democratic decline in South-East Asia, marked by attacks on the free press, rule of law and human rights. Six years under the rule of strongman Rodrigo Duterte made the country the subject of an International Criminal Court investigation of crimes against humanity. The International Criminal Court estimates the number of killings related to Duterte's drug war could be as high as 30,000, while the Office of the UN High Commission for Human Rights expressed concern over the "near impunity" of state actors suspected of carrying out brutal police operations. Despite this, polling data found that a vast majority of Filipinos remain "satisfied" with Duterte's performance at the end of his term in 2022 – satisfied enough to elect his daughter, Sara Duterte, as vice president, in tandem with Marcos Jr as president.

The continuation of strongmen legacies by electing their children to power was expected but not inevitable. Underpinning their electoral success are years of mythmaking and campaign strategies designed to enforce selective remembrance of their parents' achievements and wilful forgetting of the atrocities committed. These narratives thrive in a context where institutions for political accountability are weak and people's patience towards democratic processes has run low. But the allure of strongmen – and their descendants, for that matter – is not guaranteed. The Philippines offers a cautionary tale for the region about how people's support for strongmen is conditional, not fanatical.

2.

The Marcos–Duterte duo was announced in November 2021, six months before the elections. Prior to this announcement, there were calls for Sara Duterte to seek the presidency. The Philippine constitution prevents presidents from running for a second term – a provision designed to avoid a repeat of Marcos Sr, who held on to power for more than two decades. To work around this provision, Duterte's supporters turned to Sara to continue the legacy of her father. After months of speculation, a political alliance was forged between Marcos Jr and Sara Duterte. The alliance was backed by the political parties of three former presidents. Campaigners framed this support as symbolic of politicians rising above partisanship, while a critical interpretation suggests that it is an alliance among the country's most dominant political dynasties designed to preserve power. The Marcos–Duterte tandem called their slate the UniTeam – referring to the unification of the north, where the Marcoses are from, and the south, where the Dutertes ruled for thirty years. Owing to the popularity of their fathers, Marcos Jr and Sara Duterte were consistent frontrunners in pre-election polls.

But broader political conditions made it possible for them to accumulate power. One explanation is the weaknesses of the Philippines' institutions for political accountability. In 2021, Freedom House gave the Philippines' safeguards against corruption a mark of 1 out of 4 – a score that can be illustrated by the Marcos family's impunity from punishment. In 2018, a special anti-graft court sentenced Imelda Marcos, the wife of the late dictator Ferdinand, to at least six years in prison for funnelling US$200 million to Swiss foundations when she was the governor of Manila in the 1970s and early 1980s. Mrs Marcos appealed the decision. To remain free, she posted bail of US$7400 – roughly the equivalent of three pairs of Christian Dior shoes from her notorious footwear collection. This verdict effectively disqualified her from seeking any elective position, but it did not stop her family members from asserting their political influence. A year after her conviction, Imelda's eldest child, Imee, won a seat in the senate in alliance with President Duterte's party after serving as governor of Ilocos Norte for three terms.

How Marcos Jr would treat a body specifically designed to reclaim his family's assets remains to be seen

How Marcos Jr would treat a body specifically designed to reclaim his family's assets remains to be seen. After the 1986 People Power

Revolution, President Corazon Aquino's first executive order was to establish the Presidential Commission on Good Government (PCGG). The PCGG is a quasi-judicial body tasked with recovering the ill-gotten wealth of the Marcos family and their cronies around the world. It was this commission that prompted the Swiss government to develop a policy to return stolen assets to their rightful owners. It also influenced the UN Convention against Corruption to develop an asset-recovery agenda. The US$658 million that the Swiss government returned to the Philippines remains "one of the largest sums ever returned by any government to a country formerly ruled by a kleptocratic regime", according to the Swiss foreign ministry.

Over the years, however, the PCGG's work stalled. Of the forty-three cases it filed against the Marcos family, half were dismissed, and the rest are in progress. It recovered US$3.6 billion, which was a fraction of the estimated US$5 to $20 billion the Marcoses and their associates looted from the nation's coffers from 1968 to 1986.

The commission's future is uncertain now that Marcos Jr is president. How he would treat a body specifically designed to reclaim his family's assets remains to be seen.

To be fair to Marcos Jr, the commission's future has been in limbo long before he set eyes on the presidency. Then-president Joseph Estrada sought to move the commission under the supervision of the Department of Justice, to address its slow pace in delivering results. Under the Duterte regime, the Speaker of the House suggested moving the commission to the Office of the Solicitor General, which, at that time, was headed by a man perceived to be a Marcos supporter. Meanwhile, Duterte's budget secretary proposed the commission's dissolution as part of the government's "rightsizing" agenda. Uncertainties about the commission's future made it difficult for it to retain competent staff and recruit lawyers and asset tracers. This leads one to wonder whether the commission was set up to fail.

The weakness of institutions for accountability enabled the Marcoses to remain politically significant. After the death of Ferdinand Marcos in 1989, the family returned from exile in the United States in 1991, and they were quick to re-establish their political operations. Marcos Jr won as representative of the second district of their home town, Ilocos Norte, in 1992 and remained undefeated in subsequent elections to become governor and senator. In 2016, the Liberal Party's Leni Robredo narrowly defeated Marcos Jr in the vice-presidential race. Marcos Jr protested the outcome, accusing Robredo of electoral fraud in the island of Mindanao. The Supreme Court dismissed Marcos Jr's claim.

The 2022 presidential election was their rematch. Vice President Robredo – a public attorney and a champion of participatory governance – pulled out all stops to run a people-driven campaign to defeat Marcos Jr's well-resourced bid, which, critics claim, was bankrolled by the family's ill-gotten wealth.

Beyond the Marcoses, the 2022 election results sent a message that the Philippines has a soft spot for disgraced politicians. Marcos Jr's UniTeam includes Jinggoy Estrada, who campaigned to reclaim his seat in the Senate while he was out of jail on bail for graft and plunder charges. Former president Gloria Macapagal-Arroyo, whose tenure was marked by coup attempts and widespread protests because of corruption scandals, ran unopposed in a congressional race. "UniThieves" was how Marcos Jr's critics branded his slate. And then there is Sara Duterte, who, as vice president, now has the power to obstruct investigations into the abuses committed during her father's murderous war on drugs.

Some dismiss these developments as a matter of political fortunes. One day, you're in. The next day, you're out. One day, the Marcoses are forced into exile in Hawaii. A few decades later, they are back in the Malacañang Palace. That may be the case. But if there is one lesson that can be learned from the electoral success of these children of strongmen, it is that their political fortunes are tied to the power of democratic institutions to punish the abuses of their fathers. For now, the Philippines' institutions for political accountability have no such power.

3.

Some historians framed the 2022 election as a battle between truth and lies. In an interview with Filipino journalist and Nobel Peace Prize winner Maria Ressa, whistleblower Brittany Kaiser, a former employee of Cambridge Analytica, revealed that Marcos Jr himself approached the firm to "rebrand" their family's reputation. "As you call it historical revisionism, that's exactly what it is," Kaiser said, "but done in a data-driven and scientific way."

Marcos Jr's spokesman denied Kaiser's claim. Yet investigative reports and academic research have uncovered various ways in which Marcos supporters systematically distorted historical truths through social media. Cheryl Soriano and Fatima Gaw, media studies scholars, documented how searching for "Marcos History" on YouTube predominantly leads to channels of pro-Marcos micro-influencers who deploy creative strategies to showcase the accomplishments of Marcos Sr.

Take the case of Sangkay Janjan TV – a YouTube channel with nearly a million subscribers. The channel features the adventures of John Anthony Jaboya, or Janjan as he is called on YouTube (*sangkay* means "friend" in Waray). He posts videos of himself singing church hymns with his friends, cultivating a wholesome image that makes him a credible storyteller. One of his most watched videos – with nearly two million views – claimed that the Philippines could have taken over the United States in terms of progress if Marcos Sr's plan of building the New Society ("Bagong Lipunan") had not been interrupted by the People Power Revolution. He claimed that Lee Kuan Yew copied Marcos Sr's plan in Singapore, and that Marcos Sr was giving advice to world leaders on how to run their countries. Subscribers praised Janjan for his "illuminating"

In this online echo chamber, the Marcoses are now vindicated

videos. "When I learned the truth, and whenever I remember the sacrifices of President Marcos, I tear up," said one viewer in the comments section. "Keep up [sic] telling the truths on history of the PH," said another.

YouTube's algorithm ensures that a click on Sangkay Janjan's videos leads to recommendations to watch similar content. This includes urban legends about the source of the Marcos family's wealth (tons of gold, apparently), as well as conspiracy theories about the personalities behind the People Power Revolution. These YouTube videos, together with memes on Facebook and reels on TikTok, portray the Marcos family as victims of biased media and liberal elites who took charge of the country after the dictatorship. The Marcos name was unfairly tarnished by their political opponents, according to social media influencers. In this online echo chamber, the Marcoses are now vindicated by the outpouring of support for Marcos Jr.'s presidency from world leaders, including New Zealand's prime minister Jacinda Ardern. Ardern did not endorse Marcos Jr.

Some tech companies have made progress in addressing concerns about disinformation and platform manipulation. Twitter suspended over 300 accounts amplifying pro-Marcos hashtags because the accounts engaged in "inauthentic behaviour" or made content look more popular than it was. Meta also started addressing suspicious activities on Facebook. There were pages that had built a following for non-political posts, such as humorous memes or Bible quotes, but were renamed for partisan purposes in the lead-up to the elections. A page that posted dance videos, for example, was renamed "Bongbong Marcos news". YouTube, meanwhile, did not find these activities a violation of their community guidelines.

Tsek.ph – a consortium of Filipino academics, journalists and civil society groups – closely monitored disinformation online, long before the campaign season started. They identified Marcos Jr to be the biggest beneficiary of these tactics, while Robredo suffered the most from the attacks. She was pilloried for being out of her depth based on spliced videos showing her stuttering or making incoherent statements. Some memes tagged her as a communist sympathiser; others accused her of being a puppet of the United States. Stories were fabricated about her daughter being caught in a drug bust and a sex scandal.

While disinformation networks did the dirty work of disparaging Vice President Robredo's campaign, the official Marcos campaign's strategy was to promote positivity. Marcos Jr's speeches in rallies and interviews conveyed a single message: that unity is the solution to the country's problems. Sara Duterte told her supporters to be patient with critics who judge them for supporting the UniTeam. "If they cancel you, throw them a burger," she said, a wordplay on a Filipino adage about showing kindness when one is shown hostility.

The tenor of the Marcos-Duterte tandem is in stark contrast to Rodrigo Duterte's populist style. While Rodrigo Duterte drew a sharp line between drug addicts who need to be killed and virtuous Filipinos who need to be protected, the Marcos-Duterte tandem positioned themselves as leaders who could heal political divisions that stopped the nation from moving forward. They rejected joining debates hosted by media networks because debates, according to Marcos Jr, only relitigate issues that have long been settled. Marcos only graced one presidential debate, on a television network that endorsed his candidacy and is owned by a pastor on FBI's most wanted list for alleged sex trafficking and bulk cash smuggling. Macros Jr preferred talking directly to his supporters in campaign rallies where he controlled the stage, and in vlogs where he showed his lighter side. On YouTube, he was seen teasing his sons about their girlfriends, playing the app Mobile Legends with micro-celebrities in the gaming community, and bursting into laughter as he played the lie detector challenge with his wife. Interspersed in his vlogs was content that paid tribute to Marcos Sr. He shared anecdotes about how his father projected the nation's dignity through his sartorial choices. He talked about Marcos Sr's vision of making a great nation while showing striking images of Marcos Sr's infrastructure legacies. It is these tactics – the mundane, the playful and the sentimental – that made the Marcos family's rebranding possible. Perhaps there is wisdom in Imelda Marcos's statement in Lauren Greenfield's prize-winning documentary *The Kingmaker*. "Perception is real, truth is not," she said.

4.

Pundits have attributed Marcos Jr's victory to the elaborate network of disinformation that rehabilitated the family's image. Disinformation, the argument goes, exploited a naive and unsophisticated citizenry that cannot tell historical truths apart from electoral lies. The Tagalog term *bobotante* captures this line of thinking. A portmanteau of *bobo,* which means "stupid", and *botante,* which means "voter", the term signifies the disdain of some Filipinos for their fellow citizens who failed to vote correctly.

What counts as a correct vote, however, is not self-evident. It may seem obvious that a good voter chooses candidates with no record of corruption and a firm commitment to democratic principles. But a voter's decision-making process is more complex. Surveys found that Marcos Jr and Sara Duterte polled well across all ages and regions, except in a few provinces, including Robredo's home town in Camarines Sur. Filipino voters say both yes and no to democracy – a position that Australian political theorist Adele Webb describes as "democratic ambivalence", or the simultaneous embrace and distrust of democratic politics.

The return of democracy also meant the return of the oligarchs

In no way is the Philippines' democratic ambivalence more pronounced than in its election of Rodrigo Duterte to the presidency in 2016. It was not the "unthinking, uneducated masses" who drove Duterte's popularity, but the middle class – call-centre agents working the night shift, accountants in financial districts, Filipino nurses deployed in London – who, according to polling data, first supported the strongman. This support cannot be reduced to Filipinos giving up on democracy. Instead, it signals that democracy needs to evolve to deliver on its promised peace and prosperity. After six years of Benigno S. Aquino's reformist administration from 2010 to 2016, citizens started questioning how exactly his good governance agenda uplifted their lives. What use are transparent procurement procedures when many spent their days negotiating packed trains, kilometres-long traffic jams and congested airports? What is the point of an unprecedented 7 per cent growth rate when people cannot plan their future because of their insecure job contracts? How can families enjoy their freedoms when drug addicts on the street corner force them to stay indoors to avoid trouble?

Duterte's strongman politics tried to placate these anxieties. For many, the brutal drug war was effective in reducing criminality and curtailing the drug trade. Duterte's ambitious infrastructure program called Build, Build, Build was symbolic of a government taking people's suffering seriously by inaugurating big-ticket projects like bridges and highways that made a qualitative difference to everyday life. Under the Duterte administration, public infrastructure spending was at a record high, equivalent to 5.8 percent of the country's GDP. To date, a fifth of Duterte's flagship projects have been completed, while the rest are to be turned over to the Marcos administration.

The Marcos-Duterte tandem promised the continuity of these programs. Marcos Jr offered no concrete platforms aside from ten-minute explainers on his YouTube channel, where he talked about his plans for boosting tourism, agriculture and small businesses. But he promised to continue what the Duterte administration called "the golden age of infrastructure", invoking his father's nationalist ideology that Filipinos are destined for greatness. It was an emotive appeal that channelled the middle-class anger and frustration that had fuelled Rodrigo Duterte's campaign towards a sentiment of collective yearning for the return of the Marcoses.

"What could have happened had Marcos [Sr] not been kicked out of power?" asked Joe Galvez, a photojournalist interviewed for this piece. "What would have happened had Cory [Aquino] not been president?" Galvez, now sixty-three years old, was present in the 1986 People Power Revolution. Like many, he felt it was his responsibility to oppose the dictatorship and restore democracy. But the return of democracy also meant the return of the oligarchs, whose vested interests hijacked national progress for decades. Galvez found Aquino's leadership too weak to reign in the oligarchs and deliver on democracy's promise of political and economic equality.

Nanie Gonzales, a sixty-year-old graphic designer, shared similar views. Like Galvez, he joined the revolution. Thinking back, he said, he was too young and too "hot-blooded" to know he was "brainwashed" by liberal elites to support the popular uprising, which was "the biggest blunder in our history". Had Marcos Sr not been ousted, the Philippines would have been "on the same level as Singapore". He trusted Marcos Jr to deliver his father's grand blueprint for the Philippines.

These narratives may suggest that Marcos Jr's supporters have overlooked the atrocities that took place during martial law, as well as the recent abuses in the Duterte regime. This, however, is not always the case. Caricaturing Marcos and Duterte supporters as fanatics obscures, rather than elucidates, where the appeal of the strongmen lies.

"If you notice, people aren't saying they [Marcoses] are totally faultless," explained Jude Acidre, a congressional candidate supporting the UniTeam. He learned from his campaign experience that many Marcos supporters did not cover up or deny the human rights violations during martial law. Many chose to look the other way and embrace the spectacular legacies of the dictatorship that directly benefited their families. The same logic sustained President Duterte's popularity. While polls find that a majority of Filipinos are concerned about the human rights violations in the drug war, on balance, many consider it successful because the streets are safer now. It is not a surprise that President Duterte ended his term with a "very good" satisfaction rating.

Jude thought it was a wrong move for critics to demonise Marcos Jr and his supporters as morally bankrupt. Such judgement, he finds, only alienates people who are turned off by political bickering. Jude said that Filipinos believe the only thing holding the nation back is partisanship. A consequence of a free press is continuous coverage of activists protesting government policies and Senate hearings investigating abuses of power. Over the years, Jude said, these practices of political accountability and oversight have earned the reputation of being futile and obstructionist of progress. This is why Marcos Jr's call for unity is appealing.

Like Joe and Nanie, Jude also believed in the promise of People Power. But over thirty years, he saw his home province, Leyte, deprioritised in the national agenda. In the popular imagination, Leyte was the crowning jewel of the Marcos administration. It was gifted the San Juanico Bridge – a 2.16-kilometre architectural wonder connecting the islands of Leyte and Samar. Tour guides call it "the bridge of love". It was believed to be Ferdinand's present to his wife, Imelda, who grew up in the island of Leyte. Today, Leyte makes national headlines for devastating typhoons that hit the disaster-prone island. "People felt neglected," Jude said, and so they decided to bring back a family that has done some good for the country.

These comebacks by disgraced politicians demonstrate the uneven path of democratisation in South-East Asia

"The opposition should have presented a better idea," he added.

5.

Some observers may find developments in the Philippines troubling. But what is taking place there is far from exceptional.

The phenomenon of disgraced politicians returning to power in South-East Asia is not new. Take Indonesia's defence minister, Prabowo Subianto, appointed by erstwhile political rival President Joko Widodo. Subianto was once described by *The New York Times* as a "pariah in international affairs" and was prohibited by the Clinton, Bush and Obama administrations from visiting the United States. Yet he was welcomed to the United States for talks with his counterpart in the Trump administration, Defense Secretary Mark Esper, and received full military honours. The meeting signalled a dark day for human rights. Prabowo, the former son-in-law of late dictator Suharto, was never put on trial, but historians and activists documented his role in kidnapping and torturing anti-government demonstrators in 1998 when he was the army commander. While he is banned from returning to the military, he ran for the presidency twice and is likely to try his luck a third time in 2024.

In Malaysia, disgraced former Prime Minister Najib Razak is mounting a political comeback, as if his guilty verdict on seven counts of corruption never happened. Najib and his family were implicated in embezzling money from a multi-billion-dollar state investment fund, which led to the electoral defeat of the Barisan Nasional coalition four years ago. That was the first time the political party United Malays National Organisation (UMNO) was voted out of power since independence in 1957. Former prime minister Mahathir Mohamad described Najib's rule as a kleptocracy, one that was "far more serious" than the rule of Ferdinand Marcos Sr. Some observers claimed then-first lady Rosmah Mansor's shopping sprees of jewellery and handbags were more extravagant than those of Imelda Marcos. In 2021, Najib served as the figurehead in a state election in Malacca – a bellwether for the next election. His party, UMNO, won twenty-one out of twenty-eight seats. Like the Marcos family in the Philippines, Najib's campaign rests on giving voice to people's discontent with his successors' poor management of the economy. He reportedly hired a New York–based public relations firm to communicate his actions to American journalists, while in Malaysia he started growing his social media following and posted pictures that portray him as a man of the people, riding a Yamaha motorcycle and attending events with villagers. His supporters refer to him as "my boss" (*bossku*), a term of endearment that affirms their view of him as their leader.

These comebacks by disgraced politicians demonstrate the uneven path of democratisation in South-East Asia. The region faces challenges in institutionalising meaningful and consequential mechanisms for political accountability. There are various reasons for this. Money politics prevail in Indonesia, Malaysia and the Philippines. The cost of contesting seats in elections is prohibitive for new candidates and party outsiders, given the expectation that candidates hand out resources to local leaders, buy votes and operate "keyboard armies" amplifying campaign messages to win elections. There are certainly exceptions. Candidates running grassroots campaigns occasionally unseat established political personalities, but these cases are too sparse to become a political force that can institutionalise accountability. Instead, what takes place frequently is that politicians who competed against each other during elections form what political scientists describe as "party cartels" or "promiscuous power-sharing arrangements" to protect their interests. One could argue that Marcos Jr's call for unity among the country's political dynasties is yet another technique of colluding to avoid accountability.

Shrinking spaces for civil society and a free press also thwart democratic processes. These spaces are compromised not only by overt forms of repression, as can be witnessed in Cambodia, but also through networks of disinformation aimed to confuse the citizenry and to discredit mainstream media's reportage. South-East Asia is one of the world's most dynamic laboratories for disinformation. The term "cybertroopers" was originally used in Malaysia to describe armies of online propagandists paid to hack citizens' attentions for self-interested political ends, while a Facebook executive described the Philippines as "patient zero" in the global disinformation epidemic. At its core, disinformation tarnishes people's trust in political institutions. If everybody lies, then there is no point in going after erring public officials.

Without greater political accountability, the region will continue to be vulnerable to the ill effects of having a poor historical memory. Disgraced leaders can avoid being subject to litigation and punishment, as long as they form shrewd alliances and roll out an effective image (re)building strategy on social media.

There are big tasks ahead for advocates of democracy. An obvious area for intervention is building capacity in institutions that hold power to account, like the Philippines' Presidential Commission on Good Government. Human rights commissions, the ombudsman and citizen-driven initiatives – such as participatory audits, which boost public oversight of state-funded projects – can all assist. New institutions may be necessary to address disinformation. Tech platforms, donors and philanthropists have been attempting to take down fake accounts and unveil cyber-trooping operations, but more can be done to follow the money and hold the funders and chief architects of disinformation accountable.

Finally, as in all democracies, active listening is critical. The remarkable success of the Marcos–Duterte duo is a reminder that dismissing strongmen's supporters as ill-informed fanatics who reject democracy exacerbates hyper-partisanship at a time when bridge-building is most necessary. Citizens in the Philippines and South-East Asia are ambivalent about democracy, but this is not a risk: it is an asset. Time and again, South-East Asians have said both yes and no to democracy. If history is any guide, it is only a matter of time before they say yes to it again. ■

Dismissing strongmen's supporters as ill-informed fanatics who reject democracy exacerbates hyper-partisanship

With research assistance from Bianca Ysabelle Franco. Fieldwork for this piece was made possible by the grant "Strongmen of Asia: Democratic Bosses and How to Understand Them", funded by the Research Council of Norway (Project Number: 314849).

AUSTRALIA'S CHOICE

Can it be a bridge to Asia?

Kishore Mahbubani

Australia's strategic dilemma in the twenty-first century is simple: it can choose to be a bridge between the East and the West in the Asian Century – or the tip of the spear projecting Western power into Asia.

Different Australian governments have pursued each option in recent history. In the 1990s, when I served as the permanent secretary in the Singapore foreign ministry, we worked with Australian leaders, including Prime Minister Paul Keating, Foreign Minister Gareth Evans and Permanent Secretary Michael Costello, to draw Australia closer to the Association of Southeast Asian Nations (ASEAN). Indeed, we spoke ambitiously of creating a new community of twelve: the ten ASEAN states, Australia and New Zealand. More recently, Scott Morrison's government has swung in the opposite direction, serving as the tip of US power in Asia and adopting foreign policy positions at great variance with the choices of the ten ASEAN states.

No ASEAN country has joined the Quadrilateral Security Dialogue (the Quad), nor is any likely to do so. But ASEAN has not succumbed to appeasement; it has been treading a careful middle path, neither placating nor antagonising China, while working closely with other powers, including the United States. Australians should ask whether there is some geopolitical wisdom in the choices made by its ASEAN neighbours. And it should consider the consequences if it insists on serving as the spear of Western power in Asia.

After the May 2022 election, the Morrison government is out. With the Albanese government, a golden opportunity has emerged for Australia to undertake a strategic reset. It should grasp this opportunity with both hands.

The Asian Century

Over the past 200 years, Australia has grown and thrived in an era marked by Western domination, first by the British Empire and then by Pax Americana. As a member of this powerful Anglo-Saxon family, close to the global centre of power, Australia enjoyed many privileges. It also enjoyed an enormous sense of security as it was, implicitly or explicitly, defended by great Western powers. And when the USSR collapsed, Australia shared in the West's joyous triumphalism.

This history explains the overarching Australian refusal or reluctance to accept the most fundamental geopolitical reality of our time: that the era of Western domination is ending. Over the past few decades there has been a massive shift in power. In 1980, in purchasing power parity terms (regarded by many economists as a more accurate way to compare economic weight than using currency market conversions), China's GNP was 10 per cent of that of the United States. By 2014, China's GNP had become larger. In market terms, the US economy was eight times the size of China's in 2000; by 2020, it was only 1.5 times larger. Equally importantly, the United States was the largest trading partner for most countries in the world for many decades after the establishment of the GATT in 1947. In 2000, over 80 per cent of countries traded more with the US than with China, but by 2020 almost 70 per cent (128 countries out of 190) had more trade with China.

In 2022, with the resurgence of trans-Atlantic solidarity following the illegal Russian invasion of Ukraine and devastating Western sanctions on the Russian economy, there is a growing perception that a strong and united bloc of Western powers has returned to dominate the world order once again. The vote by 141 out of 193 UN member states to condemn the Russian invasion seemed to show a strategic alignment between the West and "the Rest". Yet countries that represented more than half the world's population, including populous nations like China, India, Pakistan, Bangladesh and South Africa, didn't vote in favour of the resolution. As a share of the world's population, 51 per cent abstained, while only 42 per cent approved.

And when the West imposed sanctions on Russia, few non-Western states joined them, with the exceptions of Japan, South Korea and Singapore. Significantly, some key friends of the United States – including Saudi Arabia and the United Arab Emirates – did not impose sanctions.

Will trans-Atlantic solidarity last after the war in Ukraine is over? Will the rest of the world continue to develop patterns and habits of cooperation outside the Western orbit? Only time will tell.

The best guess one can make is that we will see a new multipolar world order, replacing the bipolar order of the Cold War and the unipolar order of the post–Cold War era. A deep disquiet has developed in key capitals about the weaponising of the US dollar as a geopolitical instrument. Many central banks are troubled that half the assets of the Russian central banks could be seized. Hence, countries will be looking for alternatives to their reliance on the US dollar. Nothing will change right away. But if many large countries seek to carve independent space for themselves, the world will move towards a post-American, post-Western world order.

Australia refuses to accept that it needs to change course

This is where we find the greatest distance between the ASEAN and Australian perceptions of world order. Australia refuses to accept that it needs to change course. The differences are most apparent in the approach to China.

How to handle China

Superficially, there are some similarities in the way that ASEAN and Australia have adapted to the rise of China. For both, China is now the number one trading partner. In 2000, ASEAN trade with the United

States was worth US$135 billion, and its trade with China US$40 billion. By 2020, ASEAN trade with the US had grown to US$360 billion, but trade with China had exploded to US$680 billion. In 2000, Australia's trade with the United States was worth US$21 billion, and its trade with China US$9 billion. By 2020, Australian trade with the US and China were worth US$36 billion and US$160 billion, respectively.

But ASEAN and Australia have gone in opposite directions politically vis-a-vis China. Even though there have been some challenges in the ASEAN–China relationship, especially over the South China Sea (where Chinese pressure on Cambodia led to a non-agreement on the joint ASEAN communiqué in 2012), the overall relationship has developed relatively smoothly. At the last ASEAN–China summit (held virtually due to the COVID-19 pandemic), in November 2021, the two sides agreed to elevate relations to a comprehensive strategic partnership and work together on economic and trade cooperation, health and people-to-people exchanges.

Indonesia is by far the largest member of ASEAN. Traditionally, it has had difficult relations with China, and it was among the last to re-establish diplomatic relations with China, in July 1990. In contrast, Australia did so in 1972. Yet under the two last presidents of Indonesia, Susilo Bambang Yudhoyono and Joko Widodo (Jokowi), relations between Indonesia and China have grown progressively closer. Indonesia is not kowtowing to China; it is pragmatically adjusting to a new balance of power, while securing concrete dividends for its people in the process.

This explains why Indonesia participated in the Belt and Road Initiative (BRI). When Jokowi was looking for a fast train supplier for a 142-kilometre link connecting Jakarta to Bandung, he took a test ride in the Beijing–Tianjin fast train, which covers a similar distance. He was shocked that he reached his destination before he had completed his cup of tea. And his cup didn't rattle on the ride. China also offered more generous financial terms than its Japanese competitors.

Equally importantly, China was the first country to offer and deliver COVID-19 vaccines to Indonesia. By the end of 2021, Indonesia had received 215 million doses – over 80 per of its entire supply – from China. As a result, even though the two countries have continuing differences over the nine-dash line that China has drawn in the South China Sea, which includes Indonesian exclusive economic zones north of the Natuna islands, they have developed a relationship of trust, as demonstrated in the close personal connection that has developed between Xi and Jokowi.

US officials visiting Jakarta have expressed discomfort over this increasingly positive relationship. The Indonesian response is reasonable: they would also welcome American investment in Indonesian infrastructure. But little is forthcoming. US officials arrive empty-handed. It would be unwise and even immoral for an Indonesian leader to rebuff Chinese development offers that could improve the conditions of the Indonesian people. Any rational leader would make similar pragmatic choices.

The relationship that Australia should study most carefully is that between China and Vietnam. In theory, the relationship should be fraught: Vietnam was occupied intermittently by China for over a thousand years, between 111 BC and 1427 AD. Consequently, the Vietnamese are deeply suspicious of China. But over millennia, the Vietnamese have worked out a careful balance with their giant neighbour in the north. An ancient piece of Vietnamese wisdom says that a good Vietnamese leader must be able to stand up to China, but they must also be able to get along with China. If they cannot do both, they cannot be a leader of Vietnam. Over time, Australia may wish to adopt this Vietnamese wisdom.

Economic ties between Vietnam and China have flourished, including trade, which increased from US$2.5 billion in 2000 to US$162 billion in 2020. Amazingly, when Vietnam built a metro system in Hanoi, it chose to use Chinese investment and technology. Given the history between the two countries, this was unexpected. But it happened. Within the South-East Asian body politic, there is a pragmatic culture that accepts that China has been around – and will be around – for thousands of years. Hence, South-East Asians have developed the art of getting along with China.

A word on culture is critical here. In contrast to the more direct Western style of communication, most South-East Asian cultures have evolved ways of communicating subtly with each other. Showing respect doesn't mean kowtowing. But it does mean that care is taken to avoid giving offence unnecessarily. Having attended ASEAN meetings for over thirty years, I am deeply aware of the strength of this culture of mutual respect and how, over time, it has held the ASEAN family together.

Flawed choices: The Quad and AUKUS

The biggest handicap that Australians have in dealing with their Asian neighbours is that they tend to neither understand nor accept that their neighbours may have developed Asian forms of communication with each other. Nor do many Australians accept that they should learn to emulate some of these forms of communication.

For instance, most Asians believe that Australia publicly insulted China when it called publicly for an enquiry into the origins of the COVID-19 virus in Wuhan. The exact words used by Marise Payne, Australia's foreign minister, in April 2020, may have sounded innocuous to Western ears. She said: "The issues around the coronavirus are issues for independent review, and I think that it is important that we do that." Payne added, "My concern is around transparency and ensuring that we are able to engage openly." An inquiry into the origins of COVID-19 was a perfectly reasonable proposition. Payne confirmed in a speech in June 2020 that the inquiry was intended to be constructive and collaborative. But the key question was then: what is the best way to get China to cooperate? No Asian country made this request

The Quad suffers from internal contradictions that will stifle its development

publicly because they knew it would embarrass China by pushing it into a corner. To solicit China's cooperation, an Asian country would have done this privately and discreetly.

Many thoughtful and sophisticated Australians would dismiss this point. They would argue that this is about style, not substance. But given its geographical location, shouldn't Australia adapt its Western forms of communication when dealing with Asia?

Behind this question of style, there also lies a larger question of whether Australia should, in making geopolitical decisions, swim in the same direction as the South-East Asian nations or go in a completely independent direction? Should geography matter when countries make geopolitical choices?

Geography undoubtedly does matter. For instance, Canada and Mexico have to pay acute attention to their powerful neighbour, the United States. When US president Donald Trump asked, unreasonably, for the renegotiation of NAFTA, Canada and Mexico sighed and adapted. Similarly, Australia's 26 million people will be influenced, directly or indirectly, by the decisions and choices made by the 680 million people in South-East Asia, especially by the 273 million mostly Muslim people in Indonesia. Several decades ago, many hard-headed Australian strategic thinkers came to the conclusion that the most important relationship for Australia would be with Indonesia. As Paul Keating said in 1994, "No country is more important to Australia than Indonesia. If we fail to get this relationship right, and nurture and develop it, the whole web of our foreign relations is incomplete ...

The emergence of the New Order government of President Suharto, and the stability and prosperity which [it] has brought to [Indonesia], was the single most beneficial strategic development to have affected Australia and its region in the past thirty years."

Indeed, successive Australian prime ministers have made an enormous effort to preserve strong ties with Indonesia. In 1988, Foreign Minister Gareth Evans said, "I look forward to the day when the interests of Australia and Indonesia are so varied and so important that we no longer talk of 'the relationship' as though it were a patient of precarious health, sometimes sick, sometimes healthy, but always needing the worried supervision of diplomatic doctors. What matters much more than taking the temperature of our relationship is getting on with the task of building it." Yet recent Australian governments have paid little attention to Indonesian sensitivities. Australia's sudden decision to acquire nuclear-powered submarines under AUKUS would unquestionably trouble Indonesia. This was why the Indonesian foreign minister, Retno Marsudo, said on 18 October 2021: "This situation will certainly not benefit anyone ... efforts to maintain a peaceful and stable region must continue and [we] don't want the current dynamics to cause tension in the arms race and also in power projection." Morrison further embarrassed Jokowi's government by publicly calling on it to bar Russian president Vladimir Putin from the G20 leaders meeting in 2022. Such a call – which Albanese did not repeat – made Indonesia's job of chairing the G20 more difficult. No Asian neighbour of Indonesia would have tried to make life even more difficult for Jokowi.

Of course, Australia has the right to make its own decisions on foreign policy. It should be free to join AUKUS. But will such decisions enhance Australia's long-term security and prosperity in its South-East Asian and East Asian neighbourhoods? The biggest national security concern for Australia should be the danger of instability in its immediate neighbourhood, South-East Asia. How do nuclear submarines protect Australia from such instability? Recall the fall of Singapore in February 1942: the British built huge guns facing south to deter Japanese naval attacks. Instead, the Japanese came on bicycles from the north and conquered Singapore. Similarly, it will be small boats carrying refugees, not naval vessels, that will be the real threat to Australia. Nuclear submarines will be as wise a choice as the guns the British installed in Singapore. Unless they are loaded with nuclear weapons (which would be a dangerous step for Australia, making it a legitimate target for nuclear strikes), it's hard to see how they will enhance Australia's long-term security.

Similarly, it's unclear whether the Quad can enhance Australia's security, but if the Australian people believe the Quad is the answer to the nation's long-term security challenges, it should stay in and strengthen the Quad. The four current Quad leaders – Biden, Kishida, Modi and Albanese – enjoy strong personal chemistry with each other. They should continue meeting if they find it useful to do so.

However, the Quad suffers from internal contradictions that will stifle its development. First, it explicitly declares that it is not an anti-China arrangement. Indeed, China is not officially mentioned in any Quad statements. In February 2022, US secretary of state Antony

Blinken was asked explicitly if the Quad's purpose was to counter China. He stated: "This is not about standing against anyone in particular ... It is about standing up for a rules-based order, making sure that we uphold those rules and principles if they're being challenged." Yet in the eyes of the world, it is clearly perceived as an anti-China arrangement. This is why no other East Asian country has joined it: doing so would be an anti-China statement. An organisation that cannot be open or honest about its goals is at a disadvantage. The official readout of the Quad leaders' summit on 21 September 2021, stated "as Quad countries, we have pledged to donate more than 1.2 billion vaccine doses globally". Nowhere near this number have been delivered. Also, when the Quad made this declaration at the end of its meeting, all seasoned observers know that this was not why they met. The message about vaccines was meant to camouflage the real purpose of the meeting.

In the eyes of the world, it is clearly perceived as an anti-China arrangement

The second issue is that the security interests of the Quad's members are not perfectly aligned. Clearly, all four are deeply concerned about China's rise. The Australian solution is to act like the "deputy sheriff" of the United States. Australia hasn't formally sought this title, but it has stuck and no Australian government has denounced it. US president George W. Bush tried to pay Australia a compliment by calling it a sheriff. In response, the Malaysian foreign minister at the time, Syed Hamid Albar, sarcastically congratulated Australia on its "promotion". Unlike Australia, India is too big to serve as any country's deputy. It would like to emerge as a strong independent pole in a new multipolar order. And India would also prefer to see a strong Russia remain an independent pole. As a result, sharp differences have emerged between the Australian and Indian approaches to Ukraine. Australia was among the most vociferous critics of the invasion of Ukraine and imposed sharp sanctions on Russia. In contrast, India refused to condemn the invasion and did not vote for either the UN Security Council or UN General Assembly resolutions on Ukraine. India's reluctance to condemn Russia is understandable. Between 46 and 49 per cent of its armament purchases come from Russia. More importantly, the Russian veto in the UN Security Council has been the most reliable veto protecting Indian security interests in the council. During the Cold War, the Soviet Union exercised its veto six times to support India in its disputes over Kashmir and Goa.

Australia's membership of the Quad also highlights a clash between its security interests, which push it closer to India, and its economic interests, which are more aligned with China and ASEAN. Its trade in 2019 with India, China and ASEAN was worth $30 billion, $235 billion and $123 billion, respectively. These figures draw out the sharp strategic choices Australia faces. On the one hand, it could work with ASEAN to create an "inclusive" East Asian security, political and economic architecture that both includes and, implicitly, constrains China in a web of regional processes, including the East Asian Summit, the

ASEAN Regional Forum and the Regional Comprehensive Economic Partnership. Indeed, Australia is a member of these groupings. On the other hand, Australia is among the most enthusiastic supporters of the Quad, which, directly or indirectly, marginalises the inclusive ASEAN approaches. Undoubtedly, the ASEAN processes are slow and difficult. However, the group's inclusive approaches, which have involved both China and the United States in their regional cooperation initiatives, have generated four decades of peace and prosperity in East Asia, from which Australia has greatly benefitted.

We will be debating the causes of the Ukraine War for decades. Historians will argue that Europe made a major mistake in ignoring the advice of eminent American thinkers such as George Kennan and Henry Kissinger, who recommended including, rather than excluding, Russia in regional security arrangements. Kissinger, in his 1994 article calling for NATO expansion, made the following point: "A wise policy, instead of pretending that Russia has an option for NATO membership, would take two steps. It would proceed with membership for the Visigrad countries and reject a Russian veto. But at the same time, it would propose a security treaty between the new NATO and Russia to make clear that the goal is cooperation ... such a treaty could provide for consultation between NATO and Russia on matters of common interest. In such a structure, there would be no reason for Russian security concerns." Sadly, Kissinger's advice was ignored.

This was the core difference between the approaches of the ASEAN countries and that of the Morrison government in managing the return and rise of China. ASEAN believes in including China in its key regional arrangements. Morrison believes in bypassing it. It would be fair for Morrison to protest that the Chinese government has taken a hardline approach to Australia. We have a chicken and egg situation. It's difficult to ascertain who started the deterioration in relations: Australia or China. But the ASEAN governments and the Chinese government reach out to each other to manage their differences: Malaysia's Dr Mahathir did so over the East–West railway in 2019, and the Philippines' president, Rodrigo Duterte, did so in the South China Sea dispute in 2018. In contrast, the Morrison government has allowed its relations with China to deteriorate. Its approach towards China has been unwise, if not provocative. At a meeting in early 2022 with some senior ASEAN officials who had played a key role in ASEAN's development, I asked them to name their main perception of Australia's role in our region. To my surprise, they expressed that Australia is seen as a "Trojan horse" for the United States. The deterioration of relations with China is set to continue beyond the Morrison government. Even though the new Labor government welcomed a congratulatory message from Chinese premier Li Keqiang, Albanese also reaffirmed the Morrison government's view of China and its commitment to the Quad: "We will determine our own values, we will determine Australia's future direction. It's China that's changed, not Australia ... The new Australian government's priorities align with the Quad agenda."

Moving closer to ASEAN

If Australia decides – based on a hard-headed calculation of its national interests – to move closer to ASEAN in its foreign policy approaches, there are a few steps it can take to achieve that goal.

The first is obvious. On major foreign policy issues, it could, as a standard procedure, ask how close or divergent its position will be from the ASEAN position. As part of this approach, the Department of Foreign Affairs and Trade could do an audit comparing Australia's position on various international issues to the "mainstream" ASEAN position, and examine whether there are areas where Australia's position could be less divergent. This doesn't mean that Australia should adopt the dominant ASEAN position. It should work out its position based on its interests and values. Yet, having served as ambassador to the UN, I know that most normal countries (unlike the great powers) watch the company they are in when taking positions in the UN General Assembly. It's important to add that there's often no unanimity even among ASEAN countries on many questions. Singapore, for instance, will never support resolutions that question or challenge Israeli independence or sovereignty. Yet Singapore also votes for UN resolutions supporting statehood for the Palestinian people, a position which is within the international mainstream.

Australia's truculence wins it no admirers in Asia, other than India and Japan

The second step is to assess the viability of creating a community of twelve: the ten ASEAN states, Australia and New Zealand. A "community", almost by definition, requires all members to show sensitivity to each other's foreign policy preferences. It would also foster closer relationships between member states. I have seen it happen with my own eyes. In the 1990s, despite some differences between Australia and Indonesia, for example over East Timor, a close personal relationship developed between President Suharto and Prime Minister Paul Keating, as well as between foreign ministers Ali Alatas and Gareth Evans. A community of twelve is not mission impossible.

The danger of drifting apart

The suggestion that Australia and ASEAN should come together may befuddle some Australian thinkers, who see Australia standing strong and secure, anchored firmly in the Western community, especially the "Five Eyes" alliance of the five Anglo-Saxon countries (the United States, the UK, Canada, Australia and New Zealand). Its close relationship with the world's number one power, the United States, also provides the ultimate guarantee of strategic security.

It's good that this article is being written and read in 2022, in the immediate aftermath of the Russian invasion of Ukraine. The invasion has failed, partly because of a spike in Western (especially trans-Atlantic) solidarity. Western sanctions on Russia have been debilitating. The US dollar has emerged as the most powerful weapon that the West can use against its adversaries. A new sense of triumphalism, similar to the one following the collapse of the Berlin Wall and the end of the Cold War, is emerging in the West.

If indeed the West continues to dominate the world in the twenty-first century, Australia's safety and security is guaranteed. This would be the best-case scenario for Australia. However, the role of strategic planners is not to plan against best-case scenarios. And a worst-case scenario is not difficult to imagine.

Several key elements of the worst-case scenario are already apparent. As documented earlier, the relative economic weight and influence of Western powers is diminishing. Within a decade or two, China will be the undisputed number one economic power, with most countries having stronger economic ties with China than with the US. In addition, the spike in trans-Atlantic solidarity could prove to be temporary. The return of Trump or a Trump-like political leader in the United States would once again create a sharp divide across the Atlantic. Finally, within East Asia, a powerful political and economic ecosystem, centred on China's economy, could emerge.

What would be the consequences for Australia of such developments? The only way to draw out the implications is to exaggerate the consequences and suggest a truly terrible scenario (even if it is unlikely to pan out). In this truly terrible scenario, Australia would become the "Cuba" of East Asia.

There will be significant differences between the Australian "Cuba" and the Latin American "Cuba". Cuba hardly traded with the United States, whereas Australia's main trading partner is China. Yet, just as Cuba was progressively isolated from its natural political hinterland in Latin America through a combination of American sanctions and an "informal" decision by many Latin American countries to minimise contacts to avoid antagonising Washington, something similar could happen to Australia if its relationship with China remains predominantly antagonistic. Superficially, nothing will have changed. Australia will retain diplomatic relations with its East Asian neighbours. Its traditional defence and security arrangements, like the Five Power Defence Arrangements (FPDA) will remain in place. But Australia may have difficulties arranging high-level official visits to East Asian capitals. A subtle form of political isolation could envelope Australia in East Asia.

Some signs of such isolation are emerging. Curiously, even though Cuba was economically isolated from Latin America, it remained emotionally engaged, often winning admiration for its gutsiness in standing up to the United States. In contrast, Australia is deeply engaged economically with East Asia but becoming emotionally disconnected. Some Asians view Australian intransigence on China as Australia "showing off" its bravery. Yet only strong American support enables Australia to be so truculent. If US support evaporated, Australia would inevitably make the same pragmatic adjustments. Hence, Australia's truculence wins it no admirers in Asia, other than India and Japan.

Let me stress that this emergence of Australia as a metaphorical "Cuba" is not likely. I wouldn't bet on it happening. But I wouldn't bet on it *not* happening, either. The texture and chemistry of Australia's relations with many East Asian countries could progressively become more negative than positive.

Fortunately, it is well within Australia's capacity to avoid that terrible scenario. Right now, its relations with most East Asian countries are on a positive track. The Australia–ASEAN relationship remains positive. But Australia shouldn't assume that it will remain positive automatically. Australia will have to work hard to keep it positive. To achieve this, it will need to work out a long-term strategy based on a vision of Australia's role in the region. The best vision would be to position Australia as the natural bridge between the East and West. And to achieve this role, it must be accepted as a partner by both the East and the West, as ASEAN is. It can be done. ■

The best vision would be to position Australia as the natural bridge between the East and West

THE UKRAINE WAR

Does anyone want it to end?

Sheila Fitzpatrick

Every day the news shows us more pictures of apartment buildings crumbling under bombing, streets empty but for some burned-out cars and uncollected bodies, weeping women and child refugees. First it was Kyiv, then the grisly aftermath in Bucha. Then, in scenes of extraordinary devastation persisting week after week, it was Mariupol, a city that had already been pounded in the 2014 war between Ukraine and the Russia-backed separatists of the Donetsk and Luhansk People's Republics.

Every day we see President Zelenskyy personifying Ukrainian resistance and resilience in khaki fatigues. To almost universal surprise, his performance, and that of his country, has been brilliant since the start of the Russian invasion In the course of the war, his first name has morphed in the Western media from Russian Vladimir to Ukrainian Volodymyr, while his last name is making the same shift, from Zelensky to Zelenskyy. His attitude to the Russians has changed too. In mid-March, he indicated that he was prepared to drop Ukraine's application to join NATO (Russia's main demand during the lead-up to the invasion) and possibly make concessions on the breakaway regions of Eastern Ukraine. But that was when Ukraine's speedy military defeat was regarded as inevitable. Later his rhetoric hardened, with promises to fight to the end and talk of Ukrainian victory.

A supporting cast of European and American politicians shed tears of sympathy and offered secondary support (arms for Ukraine, sanctions for Russia, welcome to refugees) while staying on the sidelines. Politicians, including our own, expressed a moral outrage that is widely shared by the public, exhorting Vladimir Putin to "just stop" his invasion. But no leader who has led his nation into war can "just stop", even if he wants to (and there is no indication that Putin does). They need a way of getting out with dignity and something that can be presented to a home audience as victory, and finding that way often requires behind-the-scenes mediation. There is no sign of anything like that happening at the moment. Europe and the Anglophone world ("the West") appear united in their desire to punish Russia, but there seems to be no similar resolve about trying to end the war.

Sanctions have not crippled Russia, as some hoped. Putin is not about to be overthrown by an indignant citizenry at home, nor does a coup from within the inner circle appear likely. The Russian army, to be sure, has performed remarkably badly, and one must assume that the same was true of Russian foreign intelligence in the lead-up to the war.

We don't know for certain what Putin's real original aim was – preventing the expansion of NATO on its borders, solidifying the breakaway republics' claim to sovereignty, or guaranteeing a subservient regime in Ukraine – but, in any case, that aim has probably since changed. It cannot have been part of the original intention to focus the attack on Kyiv, with a highly visible convoy proceeding at a snail's pace along major highways towards the capital; bomb the city and its surroundings; and then pull back (leaving an array of war atrocities for reporters to photograph after their departure), before announcing that Russia would now shift its military focus to the Donbas. In mid-April, Rustam Minnekaev – the equivalent of a US two-star general, who is acting military commander of Russia's Central Military district, far from the Ukrainian fighting – threw out a teaser with his comments that Russian aims were full control of the Donbas and southern Russia to secure a land corridor along the Sea of Azov to the Crimea. He added for good measure that there was also the possibility of coming to the aid of Transnistria, the Russia-supported breakaway region of Moldova, another former Soviet republic, now independent. But there has been no authoritative confirmation of the first aim, and the Transnistria issue – prompting alarm that Putin's aggressive intentions go far beyond Ukraine – has not resurfaced.

A brief excursion into history

Western press coverage of the war tends to present a tension going back centuries between two bordering countries, Russia and Ukraine, the former being the historic bully of the latter. This projects a modern notion of nation into the past. Until the early twentieth century,

"Ukraine" was an idea circulating in the intelligentsia rather than a political reality. With the collapse of the Tsarist regime in March (by our calendar) 1917, Russia's newly established Provisional Government recognised the emergence of a small Kyiv-based independent Ukrainian state. But that proto-state failed to thrive, like its Russian sponsor, which was overthrown by the Bolsheviks in November. During the three years of Civil War and foreign intervention in the former Russian empire that followed, a variety of armies captured Kyiv and installed regimes, ending with the one established by the Russia-based Bolsheviks and their Red Army. Not all of what is now called "Ukraine" was part of this state. The Western Ukrainian regions, including Lviv, had been part of the Austro-Hungarian Empire before World War I and went to Poland in the postwar settlement, the victorious Western Allies proving unsympathetic to Ukrainian national claims.

Ukraine did well economically and politically under Stalin's successors

The Bolsheviks – somewhat unexpectedly, given their theoretical rejection of the notion of nationality, as opposed to class, as the vehicle of liberation – were more (though not wholly) sympathetic, and established a Ukrainian Soviet Socialist Republic as part of the Union of Soviet Socialist Republics in 1924 (along with the Russian Federation, Belorussia and a Transcaucasian Soviet Federative Socialist Republic, later broken up into the three Soviet republics of Georgia, Armenia and

Azerbaijan). In the 1920s, the Bolsheviks pushed indigenisation (use of vernacular language in state administration, affirmative action on behalf of non-Russian nationalities in the bureaucracy and education system) in Ukraine, as elsewhere in the union. There was local resentment of the fact that the Moscow-appointed communist leader (Lazar Kaganovich) was ethnically Jewish, not Ukrainian, and recurrent fears in Moscow that the Ukrainian intelligentsia's brand of nationalism was "bourgeois" (bad, potentially separatist, looking to the West) rather than "Soviet", Nevertheless, in Moscow's ambitious first five-year plan, introduced at the end of the 1920s, Ukrainian lobbying for heavy industrial investment often prevailed over its main competitor, the Russian Urals; and the construction of the Azovstal iron and steel plant in Mariupol (then called Zhdanov, after one of Stalin's closest associates) was one of the plan's proudest achievements.

Holodomor, the Ukrainian word for the famine that struck the Soviet Union's main grain-growing regions (Ukraine, Kazakhstan, southern Russia) in 1932–33 as a result of Stalinist collectivisation, was read by many in Ukraine as evidence of Stalin's malice specifically towards Ukrainians, and it would later become a national identity marker of post-Soviet Ukraine. By the 1930s, Moscow was generally appointing ethnic Ukrainian communists to run Ukraine – but that meant that it was ethnic leaders who, along with a large part of all Soviet republican and regional elites – perished conspicuously in the Great Purge at the end of the decade.

The Molotov–Ribbentrop Pact of 1939 brought Western Ukraine

into the Soviet Union. The whole area was overrun by German occupying forces in the Second World War. But at the end of the war, the Soviet Union emerged with its second-largest republic, Ukraine, significantly expanded by the addition of the formerly Polish western provinces, whose population were not generally well disposed to Soviet citizenship.

Ukraine did well economically and politically under Stalin's successors, Nikita Khrushchev (himself Ukrainian-born, although ethnically Russian) and Leonid Brezhnev. There was a Ukrainian nationalist wing of the "dissident" movement that developed within the Soviet intelligentsia in the 1970s and '80s, but, although much publicised in the West, it did not constitute a major threat to the Soviet regime.

Ukrainian nationalism grew during the political carnival of Mikhail Gorbachev's ill-fated reform effort in the late 1980s, but less dramatically than in the Baltic states (1940s acquisitions, like Western Ukraine) and Georgia. Accordingly, Ukraine was not among the Soviet republics most actively heading for the exit in 1990–91. As late as March 1991, 70 per cent of the Ukrainian republic's population voted in favour of the maintenance of a "renewed" Soviet Union of "equal sovereign republics". By the end of the year, however, it had become clear that the union was falling apart, and the Russian republic's newly elected president, Boris Yeltsin, led the (communist) leaders of Ukraine and Belorussia in delivering the coup de grace, taking their three Slavic republics into independent sovereignty and leaving Gorbachev – still president of the Soviet Union – presiding over an empty shell. This was already virtually a fait accompli when, a few weeks earlier, a second referendum in Ukraine had produced a popular vote of 90 per cent in favour of independence.

The Russian invasion

On 24 February 2022, after weeks of keeping the world on tenterhooks, Russia invaded Ukraine. This was accompanied by formal recognition of the sovereignty of the breakaway republics of Donetsk and Luhansk in Eastern Ukraine, but Putin's central grievance during the lead-up was NATO's encouragement of Ukraine's application for membership. This had been on the table for some years, but the Charter on Strategic Partnership between the US and Ukraine, signed on 10 November 2021, affirming US support in "countering Russian aggression" against Ukraine and accepting Ukraine's application for NATO membership, had recently upped the ante.

Russia has never shared the Western view that NATO is a benign and purely defensive alliance, even if the enemy in its war games looks like Russia. This is not just an idiosyncratic position of Putin's. When in 1989 Gorbachev decided not to act to prevent the overthrow of communist regimes in Eastern Europe (members of the Soviet-led Warsaw Pact, the East's answer to NATO), he believed he had an oral agreement with the United States and Europe that these countries would remain neutral and not be admitted into NATO. When the first Eastern European nations (Poland, Czechoslovakia and Hungary) became NATO members in 1999, then President Yeltsin was not happy, but ongoing discussions about some sort of associate membership for Russia meant there was still hope that NATO's historic anti-Russian orientation had changed). In 2004, Russia objected strongly to the acceptance of the three Baltic states – Latvia, Lithuania, and Estonia – into NATO, but at least these states were late additions to the Soviet Union, not core constituent parts. The prospect that NATO would accept the applications of Ukraine and Georgia, foundation republics in the Soviet Union, was the last straw, offensive not only to Putin but to many Russians old enough to have grown up in the Soviet Union.

The prospect that NATO would accept the applications of Ukraine and Georgia, foundation republics in the Soviet Union, was the last straw

Militarily, the war started disastrously for Russia. Putin appears to have expected that the invasion would be a three-day success story – that Ukraine would offer little resistance and that its government would fall apart, with Zelenskyy fleeing as Afghanistan leader Ashraf Ghani did after the US pull-out in August 2021. The reality has been drastically different. The advance on Kyiv, finally abandoned, became a laughing-stock for its slowness and ineptitude, and led to many Russian casualties, as well as Russian atrocities against the Ukrainian population. The Ukrainians managed to sink the *Moskva*, flagship of the Russian Black Sea Navy. It took weeks of bombing to subdue Mariupol, and even then defenders from the Azov battalion (the far-right group particularly loathed by Moscow) continued to defy the Russians from their stronghold in the basement of the huge Azovstal complex until their surrender in the third week of May. Only in the third month of the war, with the focus now shifted to the Donbas, did the Russian Army start making headway. The Ukrainian army's performance was a credit to its nation as well as to its NATO trainers. Given the economic malfunctions and corruption throughout the Ukrainian administration before the Russian invasion, it's nothing short of remarkable that the Ukrainian railways continued to function effectively, despite relentless bombing and the large volume of troops to be moved in one direction and refugees in the other.

Geopolitically, the war also looks disastrous for Russia. Sweden and Finland have abandoned a decades-long neutrality policy by applying to join NATO, which would greatly increase the length of Russia's border with NATO member states. Ukraine has not withdrawn its application to join NATO but instead has drawn even closer via NATO states' military supplies. Moldova, another former Soviet region which has neutrality enshrined in its constitution and is 100 per cent dependent on Russian gas, applied to join the European Union (though not NATO) the week after Russia's invasion of Ukraine. NATO's credibility as a defender of democracy and the values of European civilisation has increased. Its divisions over the degree of dependence of European member states on Russian oil and gas have been contained, at least so far; the invasion has made Europe, including even Germany, resolve to diminish such dependence (which means reducing a major source of Russia's export revenue) and find alternative suppliers. To be sure, the non-European, non-Anglophone world has kept its distance – not just China and India, but also, more surprisingly, Israel, a long-time US client, which expressed sympathy with Ukraine but kept aloof from sanctions against Russia, its defence minister, Benny Gantz, noting that the Western response to Russia's invasion, combining moral support with a refusal of military commitment, is a lesson to all small countries that, when the chips are down, you're on your own.

Perhaps the worst outcome of all, from the Russian standpoint, is the consolidation of Ukrainian national identity and international reputation through President Zelenskyy's very impressive military, administrative and public relations handling of the war. This applies to all Ukrainian citizens, not just ethnic Ukrainians. Ukraine's constitution, accepted in 1996, declared it to be a unitary state with a European orientation. That unitary quality, with provincial leaders appointed from Kyiv, was bound to create problems in provinces like Donetsk with large non-Ukrainian populations. Ukrainian nationalists' less than perfect record with regard to minorities, notably Jews in World War II, is part of the subtext of Russian complaints about Ukrainian "fascism" and mistreatment of the large Russian minority in the Donbas. But Russians have suffered along with ethnic Ukrainians from brutal Russian bombing (Mariupol was a Russian-speaking city in which Russians made up almost half the population before the 2014 Russian–Ukrainian conflict); and the fact that Ukraine's elected

Jewish president, Zelenskyy, has become a symbol of heroic Ukrainian resistance undermines the credibility of Moscow's "fascist" charges. Who knows? Future historians may even take the Russian invasion of 2022 as the foundational moment of a multi-national, solidly European-oriented Ukrainian state.

How is this all going to end?

US secretary of defense Lloyd Austin says the US wants to see Russia "weakened to the degree that it can't do the kind of things it has done in invading Ukraine". This implies that it is in US interests to see an outright Russian defeat (unlikely) or to have the war continue indefinitely. Indeed, applying a cold calculus to the situation, why should the United States want to stop a war that has done so much to weaken NATO's historic enemy and strengthen NATO, at some cost to the US budget (though presumably substantial profits to US military industry) but without any direct US involvement or casualties?

Zelenskyy initially wanted the war to end as soon as possible, but in the light of Ukrainian successes and the enhanced reputation of his nation as well as himself, his perspective may have changed. If the war has, as it seems, proved to be the event that finally made a Ukrainian nation, there are arguments (absent a sharp turn in the military tide against Ukraine) for keeping it running for a while. That is even regardless of any behind-the-scenes pressure from the Biden administration (which, in the opinion of some analysts, would prevent Zelenskyy cutting a deal with the Russians to end the war if he tried) and other

Western allies, on whom, at the conclusion of the war, he is going to be dependent for the rebuilding of the Ukrainian economy.

French president Emmanuel Macron periodically indicates his willingness to act as a mediator, but these initiatives have been ignored or rebuffed, at least publicly, by interested parties. The general temper is not such as to encourage peacemaking, as Pope Francis found when he tried to pair a Ukrainian and a Russian woman in the Vatican's Easter ceremonies, only to be forced to back down by Ukrainian diaspora protests.

That leaves Russia's President Putin, the man who started the war. But those who expected his intentions to become clearer at the Victory Day parade in Moscow on 9 May were disappointed. His short speech dwelt on NATO aggression (which explained why "we had to do this") and struck a patriotic note by comparing the current fighting in Ukraine to the Russian/Soviet resistance to the Nazis in World War II. With his usual agility, Zelenskyy immediately turned this back on Putin, casting Russia in the World War II "Nazi" role.

The general temper is not such as to encourage peacemaking

In the lead-up to 9 May, there was no sign that the United States or any other interested party was trying to facilitate Russia's withdrawal. Rather, the US had launched a mischievous new Putin-baiting campaign, publicly issuing instructions on how Russian citizens could make encrypted contact with the CIA when they felt like passing on useful information about their government: that is, committing treason under Russian law. Needling Putin and making life uncomfortable for Russians are all very well, but they don't contribute to bringing the violence and bloodshed of the war to an end. One can only hope that, invisibly behind the scenes, someone is trying to do something constructive to achieve that.

29 May 2022 ■

THE FIX

Solving Australia's foreign affairs challenges

Thom Woodroofe on Why Australia Should Host the UN Climate Conference in 2025

"The biggest opportunity for Australia is to use the COP to reinvent its approach to climate change, at home and abroad."

THE PROBLEM: The Albanese government inherited an Australian reputation on climate change which is in tatters around the world. In the last decade, we have gone from being perceived as a leader to a laggard. While both sides of politics are now committed to net zero emissions, neither has outlined a short-term pathway to reduce emissions that is consistent with our biggest friends and allies or that will keep global temperature increases within 1.5 degrees Celsius.

Australia's recent stance has had consequences for climate-related threats at home, as well as for our geopolitical circumstances. In the last year alone, we've experienced unprecedented floods; the United States singled out climate change as a point of contention in its relationship with the Morrison government; and Solomon Islands struck up a security relationship with China after years of disappointment with Australia – principally about our inaction on climate change.

The perennial refrain in Australia is that we can make no difference to the world's ability to tackle the climate crisis. Yet the last three decades of Australian environmental diplomacy demonstrate that when we want to make a difference, we can.

A turning point is needed to put the fight against climate change at the centre of our foreign policy, and to galvanise our industry and communities to forge a better way forward. Anthony Albanese has promised to seek to host the UN Framework Convention on Climate Change's annual Conference of the Parties (COP) in partnership with Pacific Island countries. This initiative, if approached correctly, could prove to be the turning point Australia needs.

THE PROPOSAL: Australia should seek to host the COP summit in 2025, which will be a critical year for global climate diplomacy.

The 2025 conference is the next five-yearly milestone under the Paris Agreement when all countries are required to ratchet up their national ambition, including through outlining specific plans to reduce emissions by 2035. It will be the most important climate gathering since COP26 in Glasgow in 2021 and COP15, where the Paris Agreement was adopted. This would be the largest diplomatic event ever held in Australia – its planning and execution offer a range of opportunities for Australia to interact and improve relations with other states.

Practically, partnering with the Pacific would mean that many of the dozens of smaller preparatory meetings could be held in the region, including the largest "Pre-COP" meeting, held a month beforehand. Papua New Guinea would be the obvious candidate to host the Pre-COP, given that Fiji presided over the COP itself (in Bonn) in 2017.

Ordinarily, the hosting of COPs rotates between the five UN regions. The COP in 2025 would have been on track to be hosted by the Western European and Others Group, of which Australia is a part. However, the Latin American and Caribbean Group (known as 'GRULAC') may also now have a claim to the gathering due to the one-year delay of COP26 caused by COVID-19. Expressing an early interest and, more importantly, consulting with GRULAC will be key, including with Costa Rica, which lost out on hosting the summit during the last GRULAC rotation.

Beyond the technical negotiations and political showmanship, COPs in recent years have become large industry trade fairs. As was the case at the summits in Glasgow and Paris, we could expect 40,000 delegates to attend the main two-week conference. This would likely yield a $100-million economic windfall, helping to offset a cost admittedly several times higher than that (APEC in Sydney in 2007 cost around $450 million in today's money). Due to the size of the event, only Melbourne and Sydney (and possibly Brisbane or Perth) would have capacity to host.

The government would also need to decide who would play the all-important and highly visible role of COP President. Often this is a member of cabinet (either the foreign minister or climate minister), but at times it has been a standalone ministerial role, given the huge workload and travel involved in the lead-up to build international consensus. It is important that the incumbent does not change once appointed, as so much becomes invested in their personal relationships.

WHY IT WILL WORK: History has shown that a strong COP presidency is essential for raising international climate ambition. French and British diplomacy were crucial for securing the outcomes they did. Australia is well placed as a G20 economy and middle power to do the same.

Labor has suggested it wants to host COP29 in 2024. Hosting in 2024 risks pushing Eastern Europe (of whom only coal-thirsty Poland usually puts up its hand to host) into the all-important 2025 presidency. While hosting in 2025 means Australia would risk holding the COP six months after a federal election, that is not an insurmountable concern (and may be helpful politically), as Australia's campaign for a UN Security Council seat in 2013/14 showed: the Coalition originally opposed the bid, but then embraced it once they formed government. This might, however, be an argument to designate someone as COP President with strong bona fides on both sides of politics.

But the biggest opportunity for Australia is to use the COP to reinvent its approach to climate change, at home and abroad.

If Australia can secure additional climate commitments by the rest of the world, it makes it politically easier for any Australian government to do more. Australia has often pegged its climate target to that of others, including the United States. The Biden administration, with its pledge to cut emissions by 50 to 52 per cent on 2005 levels by 2030, compared to the Albanese government's target of 43 per cent, will keep up the pressure on Australia to do more, especially with its 2035 target, which must be tabled by the 2025 summit. Some scientists have said Australia's 2035 target will need to be closer to a 67 per cent cut, which would represent a big step up. While the government is unlikely to revisit the 2030 target before 2025, hosting a major COP would pressure it to at least send a signal this target is merely a floor and not a ceiling.

Domestically, hosting the 2025 COP would provide a huge opportunity for Australians to see the breadth and benefits of climate action taking place around the world. It would also encourage greater action by our industries, businesses, cities and communities, just as it has for other host countries. Glasgow's hosting of COP26 helped the city council secure a new Green Deal, and Paris adopted a new Adaptation Plan just prior to COP21. These benefits are not short-lived. There is often an afterglow that lingers for years and leads to the development of new accountability mechanisms to ensure plans are delivered.

Finally, hosting the 2025 COP might help Australia put climate change at the centre of its foreign policy in the same way the United States, the United Kingdom, the European Union and others have. DFAT could be forced to take an all-of-department approach to the issue – including considering carbon tariffs and prioritising climate outcomes in our trade agreements, and focusing our aid spending even more significantly on adaptation and mitigation measures. This shift, alone, would represent a profound legacy for Australian foreign policymaking. ■

Reviews

Good International Citizenship: The Case for Decency
Gareth Evans
Monash University Publishing

No Enemies, No Friends: Restoring Australia's Global Relevance
Allan Behm
Upswell Publishing

FOREIGN AFFAIRS

As the geopolitical environment continues to deteriorate before our eyes, how Australia navigates a more tumultuous world while simultaneously protecting our values and interests is the question of the century.

These two books attempt to provide some answers.

In *Good International Citizenship: The Case for Decency* – an extended essay for Monash University Press's "In the National Interest" series – Gareth Evans puts forward a framework for dealing with the complexities and transnational challenges of the twenty-first century.

At the heart of this framework is Evans's concept of a good international citizen, a title he assigns to states that care about preventing and alleviating suffering around the world even when there's no direct impact on their security or prosperity. This concept guided Evans as Australian foreign minister between 1988 and 1996 under the Hawke and Keating Labor governments. In the decades since, Evans concedes, Australia's record as an international citizen has been patchy at best and is currently "embarrassingly poor".

For Evans, "It is time to take stock of why it matters to be, and to be seen to be, a good international citizen; how and why we have been backsliding; and what we can do as a nation to restore our credentials."

He opens by asking why Australia (or any other country) should care about poverty, atrocities, catastrophes and suffering in faraway countries. Evans argues that this is both a moral imperative and in the national interest.

After a short journey through his philosophical and ethical reasoning, Evans argues that we share a common humanity that obliges states to do the least harm and the most good they can. He acknowledges that the primary appeal of being a good international citizen will be to idealists. Yet for the "hard-headed realists" who want more than a "warm inner glow", Evans argues that there are three ways it is also in a state's national interest.

First, being, and being seen to be, a good international citizen enables progress on issues requiring collective action. This includes transnational and existential challenges: from pandemics to violent extremism and from ending extreme poverty to the collective action we desperately need on climate change. Second, if Australia assists another country, it will be more likely to help Australia. Third is the reputational benefit. How a country is seen by others determines how well it advances its interests. For a nation like Australia, which is not globally insignificant but not big enough to demand our interests be accommodated, soft power is particularly important. We depend upon our capacity to persuade.

Evans sets out four benchmarks for what makes a good international citizen: being a generous aid donor; advancing human rights; doing everything we can to prevent the horror of war and mass atrocities, and alleviating their consequences, including for refugees; and being an active participant in tackling large existential and transnational issues such as climate change, nuclear war and global health.

It's not much of a spoiler to reveal that Australia's record is patchy against these benchmarks. Yet Evans concludes it's not too late for the nation to become a good international citizen again and sets out – sharply and succinctly – how leaders can gain support for a more expansive and idealistic foreign policy. He explains that harnessing the power of reason is particularly important for leaders appealing to cynical politicians, advisers and public servants who are "rather immune to moral arguments". He argues that being a good international citizen is as important as promoting economic and security interests.

It's hard to see anything controversial in Evans's essay. Indeed, as we grapple with the consequences of China's increasing influence and security ties in the Pacific, few would deny the hard-headed national interest argument for greater Australian engagement in our region.

However, one wonders if it takes more to be a good international citizen in the twenty-first century. Evans's thinking is naturally grounded in his experiences as foreign minister in the 1980s and '90s, and his later role as CEO of the International Crisis Group, where he led the establishment of the principle of the Responsibility to Protect. He tends to deal with thematic issues in the international system but pays less attention to the sharpening geostrategic realities in a system characterised more by competition than cooperation. What does it take to be a better partner in this world?

This is where Allan Behm's *No Enemies, No Friends: Restoring Australia's Global Relevance* steps in. Behm, a former public servant and adviser to Labor ministers in government and in Opposition, explores the deep-seated behaviours and habits of mind that shape and limit Australia's agency as a player on the global stage and suggests how we can overcome these.

The first section of the book explores the profound insecurity at the heart of Australia's strategic mindset. For Behm, racism, misogyny, our fear of abandonment, our remoteness, isolation, distance, dependency and ongoing cultural cringe combine to shape our understanding of the world and the responses we have to it. By recognising these pathologies, Behm argues, we can address them and begin to recast our future.

Just over midway through the book, Behm dedicates a chapter to exploring conceptions of our identity, interests and values and how these manifest in our international affairs. He argues: "At this point in our national evolution, the core problem is that we do not know who we are as a nation, we do not know what we stand for as a nation, and we do not know how to articulate a set of interests that give us purpose as a nation." He goes on to explore our conceptions of national identity (and what a more inclusive identity could be), our national values, and what the ever-elusive "national interest" should be. This chapter is a timely contribution and will hopefully provoke more consideration of how we can better use our levers of power to pursue our interests and better express our values through the pursuit of these interests.

The final part of the book explores how we can design a "new international game plan" to improve our international engagement and realise our national interests. This includes reimagining and recalibrating our relationships with the United States, China, Indonesia, South-East Asia and the Pacific.

Behm holds a mirror up to Australia that will confront some and challenge almost all. He is erudite, persuasive and blistering. For this reviewer, there was much to both agree and disagree with. Behm often sweeps past perspectives and realities that don't suit his positions. For example, while he acknowledges China has "real problems with its credibility and trustworthiness", the majority of the book is dedicated to how Australia has not treated China with the respect it deserves as a great power. He places the blame for the deterioration in relations firmly on Australia and conveniently ignores evidence that doesn't suit this narrative.

No Enemies, No Friends covers a lot, and it's difficult to do justice to it in a short review such as this. Whether you agree or not with Behm's assessments, the book will force you to confront policy shibboleths, re-examine thought processes and think more deeply about how as a nation we can reckon with our past, better encapsulate our values and overhaul our foreign policy to navigate a deteriorating geostrategic environment.

Behm declares that the test of fidelity for the Australian security community is orthodoxy. Yet orthodoxy only confirms the status quo, "which is what a disrupted world is all *not* about". *No Enemies, No Friends* is Behm's provocative challenge to this orthodoxy – and it's a challenge we need more of.

At the time of writing, Australia is on the cusp of an election. If the polls are correct and we see an incoming Labor government after almost ten years in Opposition, no doubt the arguments and proposals Evans and Behm put forward – while not necessarily Labor policy – will influence how the new government responds to current international challenges. But partisanship aside, both books offer useful ideas for how Australia can exert more ambition and agency on the global stage.

Mercedes Page

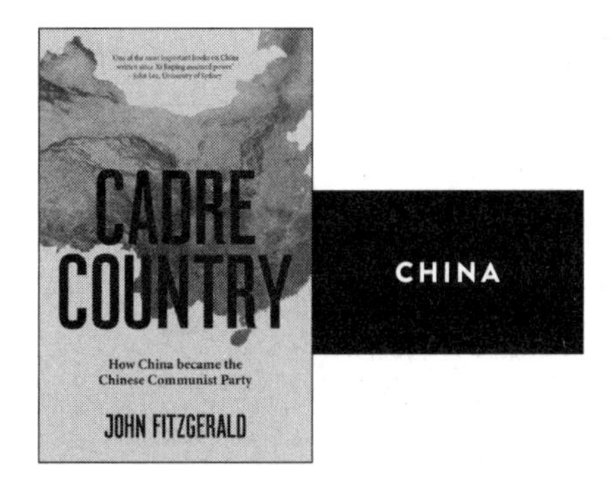

Cadre Country: How China Became the Chinese Communist Party
John Fitzgerald
UNSW Press

In *Cadre Country*, China historian John Fitzgerald argues that the Chinese Communist Party (CCP) under Xi Jinping is cannibalising Chinese society and its economy in the process of returning to its Leninist roots.

At its heart, the book is a blistering indictment of the Party's duplicity and hypocrisy. For Fitzgerald, the system of institutionalised inequality between the common Chinese and the CCP cadres – the government officials and managers employed by the Party – lies at the root of gross injustices and inequalities in China, in the past as well as today. His book takes us through the Party's attempts to shape China and its peoples in its own image through controlling social mobility, economic resources, media, language, national identity and historical narratives.

The implications for Australia and others, Fitzgerald suggests, is threefold. First, the assumptions underpinning bilateral relations with China should be re-evaluated. The relationship should be based on an informed understanding of how the Party works in the post-reform era. Under the CCP, China has changed dramatically since the heydays of reform and opening up: not only is it richer and more powerful but it is increasingly repressive at home and expansionist abroad.

Second, given China's illiberal turn under Xi, liberal democracies need to retrain the muscle memory of dealing with Leninist parties, which is something that was lost with the passing of the Cold War.

And third, we should be sceptical of the Party's claims about its achievements and version of history because they are self-serving if not all together misleading.

David Lowenthal, renowned historian and heritage scholar, in his famous book, *The Past Is a Foreign Country*, argued that the interpretation of the past is a constant process. Fitzgerald demonstrates convincingly the power of historical narratives in shaping China today, and in doing so shows us that historians have much to offer in discussions about contemporary China.

While *Cadre Country* is about contemporary China, what I found particularly helpful was Fitzgerald's historical contextualisation of recent developments in the People's Republic. The chapter on national humiliation, for example, outlines the evolution of the contested national humiliation motif through the late Qing, Republican and PRC periods, and ends with a discussion of how shame is used by the Party to fan nationalism and cement its legitimacy today.

Fitzgerald offers an insightful and at the same time simple story – insightful because it is steeped in the complexity of history, but simple in its portrayal of the Party's single-minded focus on perpetuating its power and the system of privileges for its cadres. For me, this story raises more questions than answers.

First, how should we think about the relationship between the party-state and the Chinese people? Is it between the ruling and the ruled, the oppressor and the oppressed, as suggested by Fitzgerald? An important reason for the CCP's resilience rests on social legitimacy. In fact, survey data consistently show strong public satisfaction with Chinese governments. One 2020 study, for instance, by researchers at the Harvard Kennedy School's Ash Center for Democratic Governance and Innovation, found that between 2003 and 2016, Chinese citizens' satisfaction with central and local governments increased virtually across the board. This points to a more ambiguous and complex relationship between the party-state and the Chinese people than some may think.

Second, can we attribute China's current challenges to its political superstructure? On this, I largely agree with Fitzgerald's diagnosis: many of China's problems, such as corruption, can be attributed to the party-state system. But we also should note that many of the challenges faced by China today, including socioeconomic inequality and the disruptive effects of technology, are faced by other countries, including democratic ones. The difference, of course, is that in democracies these challenges can be debated without fear of censorship or punishment by the state.

Third, how successful is the CCP's attempts to shape China and its peoples? The agency of the Chinese people is, I think, often neglected by politicians and media commentators.

From the mid-1950s to the 1970s, millions of Chinese in rural areas resisted Beijing's collectivisation policies. They resisted, actively or passively, through everyday activities such as trading on the black market. Ultimately, Mao's dream of a communist utopia was torpedoed by resistance from below.

Similarly, today, the CCP faces daunting challenges in enforcing its policies and moral values. Increasingly, the Party's conservative values are running up against social changes, including on gender, sexuality and aesthetics.

The Party under Xi Jinping may have reverted to its Leninist type, but it is far from clear whether it will be able to tame the massive economic, social and technological transformations of the post-Mao era and shape China and its peoples to its will. Even the powerful CCP is limited.

Adam Ni

Correspondence

"Reality Check" by Hugh White

John Lee

Hugh White's "Reality Check" is a gripping, fast-paced assessment of the strategic dynamics playing out over Taiwan, in which White concludes that Australia would be wiser to remain on the sidelines of any US–China conflict.

He begins with the assessment that Taiwan is a test of American credibility and that failure to defend it would be the beginning of the end for the United States in the region. As China's primary strategy to gain regional pre-eminence is to degrade the credibility of American power and resolve, Beijing has immense interest in either winning a war over Taiwan or deterring the US from entering the conflict in the first place.

Having set up the contest in this way, White proceeds to game Chinese and American options.

China, White argues, has become less reliant on economic relations with the US, and the balance of military power will increasingly be in its favour. This makes it much more tempting for Beijing to use force. The other consideration for China is how it assesses American calculations. China knows America could inflict heavy losses against its mainland through conventional means, but not enough to decisively deter Beijing or to convince Beijing to surrender. For this reason, China would expect the United States to threaten the use of nuclear weapons to deter Beijing from using force in the first place.

However, White points out that China has enough nuclear capability to destroy a dozen or more US cities, which would deter any US president from ordering a nuclear attack. Following this logic, the advantage is with Beijing. As he argues, China has a better chance of taking Taiwan without threatening nuclear war than America does of stopping China. The final piece of the argument is that China (even if it takes Taiwan) does not pose a direct or existential threat to America while the latter is not serious about genuinely containing China (even if that were possible). All this leads to the further weakening of American deterrence and calls into question the wisdom of Australia doubling down on the alliance.

This is an absorbing essay. However, the chain of reasoning passes too quickly over some key assumptions, which are incorrect or in need of much greater interrogation.

The decision to use force is informed by military calculations but is ultimately a political decision. The Chinese Community Party profoundly covets Taiwan, but its highest priority is to remain in power. This is where the non-military dimensions of a war need further assessment. Despite China's economic size and relevance, it knows the US and its allies have the economic, financial and technological means to devastate the Chinese economy without a shot being fired. The reason for Xi Jinping's "dual circulation" economic ambition and other overarching blueprints such as the Belt and Road Initiative and Made in China 2025 is that the country remains immensely vulnerable to economic devastation being unleashed upon it by the US-led advanced democracies, and such devastation would be an existential threat to the CCP's rule.

One might respond that such non-military weapons of mass destruction would also cause immense damage to the Western economies. This is true. But gaming in this context is about assessing relative gains and losses – and tolerances of these. Unlike Vladimir Putin, Xi cannot tolerate national economic catastrophe. Perhaps America and its allies have more weapons with which to deter China than White assumes.

Moreover, geostrategy is rarely decided over just one play. Even if the United States suffered the considerable blow of losing a non-nuclear war over Taiwan, it is unlikely America would simply retreat to its side of the Pacific Ocean. China has spent decades preparing for an assault against Taiwan. It is not nearly as well positioned for other theatres of conflict, something White acknowledges in arguing that China would not be able to establish hegemony over Eurasia even if it took Taiwan.

One might expect other nations to seriously build their capabilities and to dramatically increase their support for America and its allies to balance against

China. Economic and trade relations with China after conflict in Taiwan would not just snap back to normal, likely destroying Chinese plans of building gradual economic hegemony in Asia. In short, all sides must consider the possibility that our American ally is less of a lame duck than White suggests.

Finally, it is premature to suggest that allies such as Australia cannot make a difference to the military balance. For the moment, Japan is the only allied military power to have considerable impact and it has all but confirmed it would join the Americans in a war over Taiwan. Previous wargaming favouring a Chinese victory tended to assume Japanese non-involvement.

Over the next decade, Australia, Japan and others are promising to develop the capabilities required to tilt the military balance in the allies' favour, including over Taiwan. The possibility that we will fail to do so is too easily dismissed.

Dr John Lee is a senior fellow at the Hudson Institute in Washington, DC. From 2016 to 2018, he was senior adviser to the Australian foreign minister.

Lai I-Chung

Since 2021, the likelihood of China launching a war against Taiwan has been hotly debated. Two US Indo-Pacific commanders have testified that they believe a war could happen within the next six years or sooner. *The Economist* ran a cover story: "Taiwan: The Most Dangerous Place on Earth". When Russia launched an unprovoked attack against Ukraine in February, international commentators started to ask whether a war in Taiwan could be next.

The speculation is not without reason. China has long indicated that it will "take back" Taiwan someday – by force if necessary. Under Xi Jinping's leadership, Chinese acts against Taiwan have had a stronger military flavour, especially since Tsai Ing-wen came into office as Taiwanese president in 2016. China started to fly military jets near Taiwan in September 2016: first reconnaissance planes, then fighters and bombers. Since 2019, China has begun to cross the "median line" in the Taiwan Strait and to publicly deny the existence of such a line. In 2020, People's Liberation Army [PLA] aircraft conducted 370 intrusions into Taiwan's air defence identification zone. That number tripled in 2021. The PLA navy has also sent ships closer to Taiwan.

However, Xi is not considering using force only against Taiwan. China's military has harassed other neighbours, such as Japan, India and South Korea. Xi's goal is the rejuvenation of the Chinese nation by restoring what he believes to be a rightful Sino-centric order in Asia, in which China dominates, with other countries subservient to Beijing. It more or less resembles the combination of the maritime order during the Ming Empire and the continental order during the early Qing Empire.

Hugh White is right to assert that Chinese determination to seize Taiwan can't be underestimated. He is also right in saying that should Taiwan put up a good defence, with or without the direct assistance of the United States, Xi could resort to more drastic measures, including the threat of nuclear weapons. We witnessed similar developments lead to a nuclear threat from Russia in its war on Ukraine. But when he argues that war in the Taiwan Strait can be localised and treated as a merely bilateral affair between China and Taiwan, and that Australia should make it clear to the United States that Australia has no business there, in the hope that doing so would dissuade Washington from getting involved, I believe he is underestimating the regional, and even global, nature of such a war.

For China, seizing Taiwan means three things. First, China wants to eradicate any last hope that democracy can survive in a Chinese nation. Xi has long boasted that the Chinese state represents an alternative – viable – governing model to democracy. Taiwan's existence as a democracy is a direct rebuttal to that assertion, challenging Xi's contention that the current democratic orthodoxy is culturally biased and is no fit for a Chinese nation.

Second, seizing Taiwan would give China control over Taiwan's prized high-tech industrial power. Advanced computer chips produced in Taiwan have become an essential part of the new 5G era. Despite China's huge investments in its semiconductor industry, it cannot manufacture the advanced, high-quality chips that Taiwan provides to the world. Seizing Taiwan would give China control of an advanced semiconductor technology base and more powerful leverage against Western powers, especially the United States.

Third, annexing Taiwan would give China an immense strategic advantage in the Indo-Pacific. China could effectively cut off North-East Asia from South-East Asia, and the underwater geography along eastern Taiwan would give Chinese submarines unimpeded access to the entire Pacific Ocean, all the way to the western shores of the United States. Conquering Taiwan, which possesses one of the biggest natural islands, Itu Aba, in the South China Sea, would give China a naturally habitable strategic asset, making it more difficult for other countries to maintain a free and open sea lane in the region.

Xi understands the critical value of Taiwan. He has indicated that unification is core to achieving the "great rejuvenation of the Chinese Nation". The enormous stakes that surround Taiwan mean that a war in the Taiwan Strait cannot be localised, as White hopes. Conflict over Taiwan is no longer simply a bilateral affair. This is one reason why the security of the Taiwan Strait now receives so much attention from countries and groupings such as Japan, South Korea, the G7 and the European Union, as well as the United States. Statements from the Morrison government indicated that it also appreciated that reality.

Should Beijing invade, Taiwan will defend itself with everything it has, with or without Australia's assistance or involvement. Australia's choice in such a scenario would reflect how it understands this war and what kind of regional order it chooses to uphold.

Lai I-Chung is the president of the Prospect Foundation, Taiwan.

Derek McDougall

In "Reality Check", Hugh White provides thought-provoking analysis of the likelihood and consequences of war over Taiwan. War would be a tragedy not only for the people of Taiwan. The ramifications would extend to other countries directly or indirectly involved, including Australia.

While I do not disagree with White about the likelihood of war, I think his discussion of the consequences requires qualification. His portrayal reminds me of the domino theory, as advanced during the Vietnam War in the 1960s: if one domino falls, then all the dominoes fall. In this case, Taiwan takes the place of South Vietnam.

But would the "fall" of Taiwan really mean a complete realignment of geopolitics in the region? Is the United States going to become a spent force, with its allies and other powers subject to Chinese hegemony? Similarly, if China backed off in the event of conflict over Taiwan, would "its claim to America's position in Asia . . . collapse"?

In either case the power suffering the reverse would be weakened, but not to the extent of crumbling or collapsing. If the United States were to suffer the setback, it would still retain significant influence. US allies and partners might put less emphasis on their relationships with Washington, but those relationships would remain important. US relations with Japan and South Korea, its key allies in North-East Asia, are likely to become weaker but not collapse. Both countries would become more independent, facing pressure to seek accommodation with Beijing while using the (weakened) US relationship as a means of enhancing their own agency.

Similarly, in South-East Asia most countries attempt "soft balancing with accommodation" in their relations with China. Singapore is a de facto US security partner, while on good terms with China; Vietnam is the most assertive South-East Asian country in its dispute with China over the South China Sea. The Philippines is close to the US, but this relationship can vacillate. Governments in the Philippines have been deferential towards China, while the public is generally sceptical about Beijing's intentions; the armed forces have strong links to the US. In the event of the "fall" of Taiwan, South-East Asian countries will move closer to China while retaining significant but reduced relationships with the US. It is a matter of degree.

Success for China over Taiwan would be a negative development for India, but there are many dimensions to the Sino-Indian relationship. In line with its strategy of multi-alignment, India would likely maintain its relationship with the United States.

Similarly, if China had to step back, it would no doubt attempt to rebuild its relationships with a range of powers in the region.

In the event of a Sino-US war over Taiwan, White's view is that Australia has "nothing to gain and much to lose". Nevertheless, he expects Australia to side openly with the United States. "Much to lose" for Australia relates to White's expectation that the US could not win a military contest over Taiwan. A loss, he argues, would have a huge impact on US credibility, destroying its strategic position in Asia, including the US–Australia alliance; Australia would have to work out its relationship with China on its own.

While I agree that Australia should not become involved militarily in a Taiwan conflict, I think White's predictions about the consequences for Australia of such a crisis are too dire. If the United States is defeated or suffers a major setback, that does not necessarily mean the end of the US–Australia alliance. The US is likely to remain a strong focus for Australia's international engagement, whether the alliance becomes diminished or even disappears.

For the US, the need to build coalitions on a range of issues, not to mention its direct stake in Australia's economic and security affairs, will mean continued attention to US–Australian relations.

Allowing for some exaggeration in White's analysis of the consequences of a major crisis over Taiwan, it would still be judicious to minimise the chances of such a situation arising. I agree with White that "Taiwan must work out its future relationship with Beijing as best it can". While the Hong Kong precedent does not augur well, Taiwan has a much stronger negotiating position than Hong Kong had. The US, Australia and other interested nations should encourage exploration of possibilities, rather than allowing unrealistic illusions to persist.

While White's analysis of the consequences of a crisis over Taiwan is realistic and compelling, predicting the worst-case outcome can actually lead to the worst-case outcome.

Derek McDougall is a professorial fellow in the School of Social and Political Sciences, and a research affiliate in the Peacebuilding Initiative, University of Melbourne.

Mark Harrison

For decades, Australian foreign policy analysis has been dominated by a style that could, for want of a better term, be labelled "realist". It holds that mature accounts of Australia's international relations should proceed from the reality of the power of states in the international system and calculations of the national interest. Accordingly, it sees the foundational task for maintaining Australia's prosperity and security as managing relations with the great powers: the United States and China. This position is so normalised that it hard to see it as anything other than a self-evident truth.

This realist-dominated analysis has led to a consensus about the contemporary task for Australia's foreign policy: Australia must accept, or embrace, the reality that China, a rising power, will exercise a greater degree of hegemony in the region and that US regional power will diminish proportionately.

With Taiwan, as Hugh White's essay shows, this dominant analytical style becomes sharply visible. China claims Taiwan as its territory and the rise of the People's Republic means it will inevitably take over the island. This may happen either peacefully or militarily, in which case, US involvement is likely. It is in Australia's interests for any takeover to be peaceful.

Realist analyses have a closed-loop logic: they proceed from an epistemological commitment to reducing international relations to metrics of state power and validate their analyses with real-world policy proscriptions that assume that international relations can be so reduced.

But, conceptually speaking, these analyses do leak. National politics, cultures and identities push their way in at the margins, and raise questions that require work to exclude. For Taiwan, these analyses discount, and usually do not even register, the century-long pursuit by the Taiwanese people of sovereignty and democracy. Neither do they interrogate the complex ideological architecture of the CCP's claim over Taiwan, nor account for Beijing's Taiwan policy failures over seventy years.

Furthermore, although realism's proponents claim to eschew morals and values as distractions from clear-eyed policymaking, morality sits at the centre of these analyses. Realists claim that allowing values to dictate foreign policy leads to short-term decisions favouring partisan causes. But implicit in this is a moral opinion – that outcomes guided by values will be worse than those grounded in the reality of state power.

For realists, a policy of defending Taiwan is a moral judgement that will lead Australia into a far larger and more terrible conflict than simply accepting an inevitable PRC takeover. While Taiwan's democracy would be extinguished, and this would be regrettable, it is morally better than the alternative.

And the alternative usually put forward is nuclear war. Australian realist analyses of the future of Taiwan are fixated on a large-scale cross-Strait conflict, and especially on the use of nuclear weapons by the United States and China.

Beijing has never threatened to use its nuclear arsenal. It has never suggested that it is willing to sacrifice Shanghai or Guangzhou in the cause of unification. In fact, Beijing has said almost nothing at all about how it plans to take Taiwan. It offers Taipei the non-negotiable outcome of One Country Two Systems with no roadmap to get there. Beijing's Taiwan policy is a black box that remains scarcely examined in Australian foreign policy analysis.

But brandishing the righteous cause of averting nuclear war validates Australian realism's analytical integrity and its implicit moralising. It also shows that the moral force of the sovereignty and democracy of the Taiwanese people is strong enough that it takes invoking Armageddon to justify setting them aside.

Yet when analyses are more interested in their own internal logic than in offering meaningful insights into states, peoples and decision-making, when they deliberately disconnect from the lives in Asia over whose future they righteously and uncomprehendingly pronounce, then perhaps they are more about Australia's national preoccupations than the realities of a changing world.

Australian foreign policy realism is part of a national policy life that has spent the last forty years fetishising great states and great markets. Its fixation on global power has always expressed Australia's anxiety about its place in the region and its post-imperial identity. The future of Taiwan in this worldview – the "Taiwan choice", not "Taiwan's choice" – is seen as Australia's choice between the United States or China, the past or the future, clutching the apron-strings of empire (whether British or American) or finding a place in Asia. Australian realism has always had an urgent tone that is as much political manifesto as policy analysis.

But this tired, insular national preoccupation has never properly considered the histories, cultures and politics of the region. In the Xi era and post-Trump, and confronting the horrors of Ukraine, these realist policy declarations no longer answer the questions our nation faces. China's power is no longer in doubt, and as a result Australia faces myriad difficult questions, including about the future of the Taiwanese people and the Taiwan they cherish, for which the old answers of lurid visions of the great China market or moralising acquiescence to PRC state power are simply inadequate.

Australia needs generational change in its foreign policy analysis. The current state of this analysis is ossified, complacent and unwilling to address its own contradictions. The weight of its moralising fatalism, presented in White's essay with the objective authority of a "reality check", has over time come to diminish Australia's national life. There are no easy choices for Australia, but basing our choices on an accounting of the region's peoples and their aspirations might allow us to achieve our own aspirations for a prosperous and secure future in a changing world order.

Mark Harrison is senior lecturer in Chinese studies at the University of Tasmania.

Hugh White responds

These four interesting and insightful commentaries present a valuable spread of responses to my essay. John Lee thinks US deterrence of a Chinese attack on Taiwan is more robust than I do. Lai I-Chung thinks the wider international community has a bigger stake in protecting Taiwan's status quo than I do. Derek McDougall thinks the stakes in a Taiwan crisis for America's position in Asia and the US-Australia alliance are less serious than I do. And Mark Harrison thinks my analysis gives insufficient weight to the aspirations of the people of Taiwan.

Let's start with John Lee's arguments that America's position vis-a-vis China is stronger than I suggest. I think he accepts that America's chances of winning a war over Taiwan have dwindled to the point that its ambiguous threats to fight for Taiwan are no longer sufficient. He argues, however, that there are four other factors which would help deter Beijing.

First, he mentions the economic costs of the massive sanctions, which, in the wake of the Western response to the Ukraine crisis, Beijing must expect to suffer if it attacks Taiwan. I think that is a good point. The essay was written before Ukraine was invaded, and hence before the scale of Western sanctions on Russia was known. I'm sure that China's leaders are taking careful note. No doubt Russia's economic punishment has strengthened the arguments for Beijing to stick with the status quo over Taiwan. Whether it has strengthened them enough to counteract the arguments in favour of a move against Taiwan is a different question. As Lee mentions, China is harder to sanction than Russia, and more resilient, so I wouldn't bet on it.

Second, Lee thinks America could open other military fronts against China in places where Beijing is less well prepared to prevail than Taiwan. I'd be interested to know what fronts he has in mind. I'll confess I can't think of any. I can't imagine, for example, that America would choose to fight China in Central Asia or the Himalayas.

Third, he suggests that a Chinese attack on Taiwan would push other countries in Asia to increase their support for America, to China's detriment. I think the opposite outcome is more likely. As I explain in the essay, there is little chance that America will succeed in defending Taiwan, and failure would gravely damage US credibility, making other countries less inclined to look to America, and more willing to accommodate China's claims to regional primacy.

And fourth, Lee thinks that I underestimate the help that allies such as Japan and Australia might provide to America in a war over Taiwan. They are the only two regional allies that are even remotely likely to answer America's call to join a war against China. Nothing in Australia's current defence plans will deliver capabilities that could make any material difference to the outcome of a war in the Taiwan Strait – including the nuclear-powered subs. And while Japan is better armed than us, their forces would not fundamentally change the course of battle, and despite bold talk from some leaders, Japan's willingness to go to war remains untested and, I think, uncertain.

The question of whether other countries might get involved leads us to Lai I-Chung's commentary. He suggests that I view the Taiwan issue too narrowly as a contest between America and China. He says the ideological, technological and geostrategic consequences of a Chinese seizure of Taiwan would be significant for many other countries as well. That means a war in the Taiwan Strait could not be localised, because other countries would be drawn into the fight. I do not think that is right. I agree that many other countries have interests in the status quo being maintained, as we can see from the attention the issues receive in official communiqués – as Lai mentions. But communiqué language is cheap. I do not believe those other countries' interests would be strong enough to compel them to go to war to defend Taiwan. A Chinese takeover of Taiwan would indeed have serious consequences for many countries – but not as serious as going to war with China.

In a somewhat contrary vein, Derek McDougall argues that the consequences would be less serious than I do. He thinks that the "loss" of Taiwan would diminish but not destroy America's strategic position in Asia. Alliances with South Korea, Japan and Australia would be weakened but survive, he suggests, and South-East Asians would still look to America to balance China. I think that underestimates how seismic that failure would be – and how fragile the foundations of those alliances really are. They depend on US allies' willingness to trust America to defend it, and I think a US failure to defend Taiwan would erode that trust – already under strain – below the critical point at which Japan, in particular, decides it must at long last look to its own defence, for example by acquiring its own nuclear weapons.

Which brings us to Mark Harrison's criticism. He says that I fail to take due account of the views of the Taiwanese themselves. He attributes this failure to my attachment to the realist school of international relations. Actually, though I'm not much of a one for doctrinal debates, I've always found the English school of Bull and Wight more congenial than the realism of Morgenthau and Mearsheimer. But I own to being a realist to this extent: I try to focus on the real choices that governments and peoples must make as they navigate the international system, and to take account of the full range of factors that bear on those choices.

That is why, like Harrison, I think it is a mistake to focus exclusively on power and force, as Morgenthau et al. tend to do, and ignore the important issues that Harrison mentions. But I think Harrison makes a similar mistake when he goes the other way and excludes questions of power and force from his analysis – and especially when he ignores the risks and consequences of war. Thus, while I agree that the aspirations of the Taiwanese people must weigh in the balance as we in Australia, and others in America and elsewhere, decide how to respond if China decides to use force, I think we must weigh the consequences of war too.

The risk of war over Taiwan is very real, so the choice we face is between two grave evils. On one side, the suppression of Taiwan's democracy and the subjugation of its people. On the other side, a major war, quite probably a nuclear war, which would not save the people of Taiwan but would inflict terrible suffering on them and on many others.

Only if we leave the question of war out of our deliberations is it easy to decide that we should unconditionally support the Taiwanese in fulfilling their aspirations. When the issue of war is considered, the choice becomes much harder. So I'd simply ask: if China decides to use force to take Taiwan, should we go to war or not? It is a simple and very important question which deserves a clear answer. My answer is "no". If Harrison's answer is "yes", I'd be interested to hear his reasons.

Hugh White is an emeritus professor of strategic studies at the Australian National University.

Subscribe to Australian Foreign Affairs & save up to 28% on the cover price.

Enjoy free home delivery of the print edition and full digital as well as ebook access to the journal via the Australian Foreign Affairs website and app for Android and iPhone users.

Forthcoming issue:
The Return of the West
(October 2022)

Never miss an issue. Subscribe and save.

☐ **1 year auto-renewing print and digital subscription** (3 issues) $49.99 within Australia. Outside Australia $79.99*.

☐ **1 year print and digital subscription** (3 issues) $59.99 within Australia. Outside Australia $99.99.

☐ **1 year auto-renewing digital subscription** (3 issues) $29.99.*

☐ **2 year print and digital subscription** (6 issues) $114.99 within Australia.

☐ **1 year auto-renewing digital Quarterly Essay and Australian Foreign Affairs bundle subscription** (7 issues) $69.99.*

☐ Tick here to commence subscription with the current issue.

Give an inspired gift. Subscribe a friend.

☐ **1 year print and digital gift subscription** (3 issues) $59.99 within Australia. Outside Australia $99.99.

☐ **1 year digital-only gift subscription** (3 issues) $29.99.

☐ **2 year print and digital gift subscription** (6 issues) $114.99 within Australia.

☐ **1 year digital-only Quarterly Essay and Australian Foreign Affairs bundle gift subscription** (7 issues) $69.99.

☐ Tick here to commence subscription with the current issue.

ALL PRICES INCLUDE GST, POSTAGE AND HANDLING.

*Your subscription will automatically renew until you notify us to stop. Prior to the end of your subscription period, we will send you a reminder notice.

Please turn over for subscription order form, or subscribe online at **australianforeignaffairs.com**
Alternatively, call 1800 077 514 or +61 3 9486 0288 or email **subscribe@australianforeignaffairs.com**

Back Issues

ALL PRICES INCLUDE GST, POSTAGE AND HANDLING.

- ☐ **AFA1** ($15.99) The Big Picture
- ☐ **AFA2** ($15.99) Trump in Asia
- ☐ **AFA3** ($15.99) Australia & Indonesia
- ☐ **AFA4** ($15.99) Defending Australia
- ☐ **AFA5** ($15.99) Are We Asian Yet?
- ☐ **AFA6** ($15.99) Our Sphere of Influence
- ☐ **AFA7** ($15.99) China Dependence
- ☐ **AFA8** ($15.99) Can We Trust America?
- ☐ **AFA9** ($15.99) Spy vs Spy
- ☐ **AFA10** ($15.99) Friends, Allies and Enemies
- ☐ **AFA11** ($15.99) The March of Autocracy
- ☐ **AFA12** ($15.99) Feeling the Heat
- ☐ **AFA13** ($22.99) India Rising?
- ☐ **AFA14** ($22.99) The Taiwan Choice

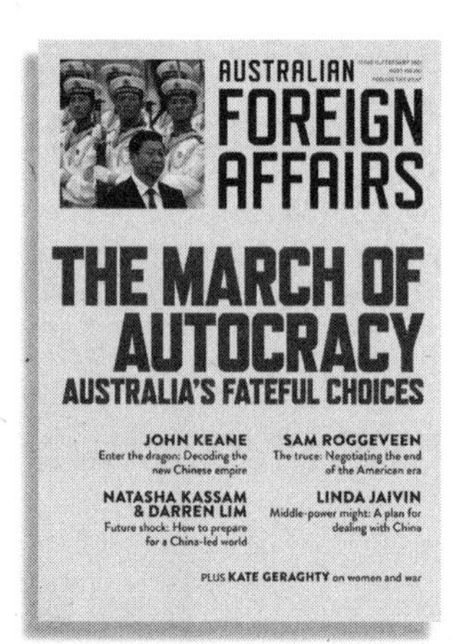

PAYMENT DETAILS I enclose a cheque/money order made out to Schwartz Books Pty Ltd.
Or please debit my credit card (MasterCard, Visa or Amex accepted).

CARD NO. ☐☐☐☐☐☐☐☐☐☐☐☐☐☐☐☐

EXPIRY DATE / CCV AMOUNT $

CARDHOLDER'S NAME

SIGNATURE

NAME

ADDRESS

EMAIL PHONE

Post or fax this form to: Reply Paid 90094, Collingwood VIC 3066 **Freecall:** 1800 077 514 **or** +61 3 9486 0288
Fax: (03) 9011 6106 **Email:** subscribe@australianforeignaffairs.com **Website:** australianforeignaffairs.com
Subscribe online at australianforeignaffairs.com/subscribe (please do not send electronic scans of this form)

Australian Foreign Affairs has a new app for Android and iPhone users

Access the entire Australian Foreign Affairs collection • Read extracts and latest news • Save essays to read offline • Adjust font size, manage your subscription and toggle between light and dark reading modes
Download an ebook for your preferred device

AUSTRALIANFOREIGNAFFAIRS.COM/APP

The Back Page

FOREIGN POLICY CONCEPTS AND JARGON, EXPLAINED

DIGITAL DIPLOMACY

What is it: An awkward term with a lot of near-analogues. Cyber diplomacy, digital diplomacy, digiplomacy and ediplomacy have all been used, not very precisely.

So what's the difference: One distinction is that digital diplomacy refers to diplomacy that uses digital techniques, while cyber diplomacy deals with diplomatic issues arising from information technologies.

Where does it come from: Digital diplomacy first attracted attention in the late 1990s, then gained slow momentum in response to the September 11 attacks. In 2002, a Taskforce on eDiplomacy was established by Colin Powell (Secretary of State, US president George W. Bush). It was later renamed the Office of eDiplomacy. Nevertheless by 2009, it had as few as six members of staff.

Isn't it just a form of cultural diplomacy: Some people think so. When Hillary Clinton (Secretary of State, US president Barack Obama) announced a technology-driven "21st Century Statecraft", which included plans for a "Civil Society 2.0", it attracted criticism. In *Foreign Affairs*, Emmanuel Yujuico (research fellow, London School of Economics) and Betsy Gelb (professor, University of Houston) called it "social engineering" destined to fail.

Does it work: So many different things get called "digital diplomacy" it's hard to say. In a 2010 speech, Hillary Clinton, arguably the most influential figure in digital diplomacy, joked that "even in established democracies like the United States, we've seen the power of these [social networking] tools to change history. Some of you may still remember the 2008 presidential election here". In 2016, "her emails" and their reception on social media then helped change the course of another election.